PROSPERITY EDUCATION

ENGLISH COLLOCATIONS IN CONTEXT

B2 – C1

David Bohlke

Registered offices: Sherlock Close, Cambridge
CB3 0HP, United Kingdom

First published 2022

ISBN: 978-1-913825-66-9

Cover design by ORP Cambridge

For further information and resources, visit:
www.prosperityeducation.net

To infinity and beyond.

Contents

Introduction

If you've been studying English even for a short period of time, you've probably already come across a *considerable number* of collocations. Perhaps you encountered some the last time you *sat for an exam*. Are you confident that you're learning them correctly? Or do they make you *hopelessly confused*? Is it hard for you to *make time* to really learn them? Well, this *user-friendly* book *takes an in-depth look* at collocations.

What are collocations?

Collocations are groups of two or more words that tend to be used together. They are common in English and sound 'right' to native speakers. Examples include *heavy rain*, *make a decision* and *wildly optimistic*. If a speaker instead says *large rain, do a decision* and *excitedly optimistic*, the listener will likely understand the gist of what's been said, but the phrases will sound strange – even wrong. A native speaker would never combine words in this way.

There is not always a grammatical reason why some words go together in English while others do not. That is what makes learning and remembering collocations a challenge. There is often not a clear reason why a native speaker says *fast food*, for example, but not *quick food*.

Another reason why learning collocations can be a challenge is that many words in English have several collocations. For example, the word *friend(s)* can be used in *true friend*, *trusted friend, long-lost friend, circle of friends, make friends, meet through friends, send a friend request* and in many other ways too.

Why learn collocations?

When you learn collocations your language will sound more natural, and you will be more easily understood. Using collocations correctly will help to show others your true level of English. And if you know a lot of collocations, you will also have multiple ways of expressing yourself!

In addition, a good knowledge of collocations will help you if you are preparing to take standardised exams like IELTS or TOEFL. Collocations are common in these types of exams. If you need to speak or write as part of an exam, your language will sound much more natural if you use collocations correctly.

Types of collocations

There are many types of collocations. Some of the most common types are:

adverb + adjective	I think he's *painfully shy*. I've been *incredibly busy* lately. My classmates are *exceptionally friendly*.
adjective + noun	The father is often the *main breadwinner*. What I'm offering has a *competitive advantage*. A *common thread* in her work is the use of colour.
noun + noun	I have *brand loyalty* for certain things. I'd start by thinking about your *target audience*. A community family is not made up of *blood relatives*.
verb + noun	At night we might *do a puzzle*. They often *slash prices* on big-ticket items. Don't feel pressured to *declare a major* right away.
verb + adverb	I don't think he *dresses appropriately*. She *works tirelessly* during the week. Look, I *control* it *remotely*.
verb + prepositional phrase	The house *is in the suburbs*. Make sure you *are on time*. That style of dress *is in fashion*.
adjective + prepositional phrase	She's *low on cash*. I'm not *active on social media*. I've been eating a lot of food that is *high in fat* lately.

Learning collocations

When you come across a new collocation, think of it as a 'chunk' of language. It's easier for our brains to remember and use language in chunks rather than as single words.

Here are some other tips that may be helpful in learning collocations:

- Read a lot. It's an excellent way to see collocations in context.

- Try to recognise collocations when you see or hear them.

- Use coloured highlighter pens to mark different types of collocations.

- Write down other words that collocate with the new collocation.

- Practise using new collocations soon after learning them.

How to use this book

This book can be used as a classroom text, but it's primarily a book for self-study. It contains 40 units on everyday topics commonly found in coursebooks. In the odd-numbered units, the collocations are presented through two dialogues. In the even-numbered units, the collocations are presented through a variety of texts.

Each unit presents approximately 15 collocations in context. It's suggested that you first read the dialogues and texts, and then try to use the context to guess any unfamiliar collocations. If you cannot guess, check their meaning in a dictionary. Feel free to make notes on the dialogues and texts, and in the margins.

Try to learn each whole collocation, but pay attention to the individual words. After you have read and understood the dialogues/texts, move onto the two self-check exercises. Refer back to the collocations in the dialogues/texts as needed. Once you have completed the self-checks, check the Answer key at the back of the book (pages 113–122).

If you choose to keep a separate vocabulary notebook, note down any new collocations. You may wish to organise them by topic or by structure.

Within the appendices, there is a section named **Collocation expansion** (pages 123–133), which features additional collocations related to each unit's topic. These are not practised in the book, but it's a good idea to look over these collocations as well. This book contains more than 2,200 collocations when these are included, all of which are indexed on pages 141–161.

Additional ideas for self-study

- Create a mind map. Draw lines from the topic and list the collocations.

- Write true sentences. Use the collocations in personalised sentences.

- Draw pictures. Create a literal representation of each collocation.

- Create flash cards. Write a collocation on one side and its definition on the other.

- Write your own conversation. Make up a dialogue that contains several collocations in context.

- Do a news search. Find real-world examples in the News sections of your search engine.

- Test yourself. Create a quiz on the collocations, and then take it a few weeks later.

Unit 1
Friends

Costas:	How's college life so far?
Jill:	It's great.
Costas:	Have you **made friends**?
Jill:	Sure. My classmates are **exceptionally friendly**. But I haven't really made friends with anyone in my dorm. They are **not particularly friendly**.
Costas:	Really?
Jill:	I mean, they're nice enough but there isn't anyone I would consider a true friend. I talk to everyone and I want people to like me, but it's hard.
Costas:	Can I give you some **friendly advice**?
Jill:	Of course.
Costas:	Don't try so hard. Just be yourself. It can take time to **develop a friendship**.
Jill:	I suppose. It's not that I don't know people here. I have a lot of **casual acquaintances**. And I have a couple of friends from high school here as well, so we get together sometimes.

Lacy:	Have you seen Chris lately?
Ian:	I haven't talked to him in ages. Actually, we're not **on speaking terms**.
Lacy:	What? What happened? You guys used to **get on famously**.
Ian:	I know. We hung out almost every weekend. He was a very **close friend**. Then we had a huge falling out. It's a long story, but basically he **divulged a secret** I had told him, and then said he didn't.
Lacy:	That's sad to hear. Things like that can really **destroy a friendship**.
Ian:	It's so true. I was hoping we could somehow **repair our friendship**, but that seems more and more unlikely unless he reaches out to me.
Lacy:	So you never see him?
Ian:	Well, I do **cross paths with him** from time to time because we have the same **circle of friends**. We just avoid each other.
Lacy:	Well, hopefully he'll come around.
Ian:	Thanks. I hope so, too.

Self-check 1

Circle the correct words.

Do you want to **1) make / develop** friends at university? Maybe these tips can help …

- Start friendly conversations with the people you cross **2) friends / paths** with at school and get to know them. They may start out as **3) speaking / casual** acquaintances, but in time they may become **4) friendly / close** friends.

- Join a club. It's a great way to enlarge your circle of **5) advice / friends**. If someone is not **6) famously / particularly** friendly for some reason, don't worry. Find someone who is and get to know them.

- Don't rush things. It won't be helpful to push too hard because you will just come across as needy. It takes time to **7) develop / divulge** a friendship.

Self-check 2

Complete the descriptions with words from the box. Two words are not used.

destroy	divulge	exceptionally	famously	friend
friendly	make	repair	speaking	true

1 I want to be friends again. Do you think there is any way we can _____ our friendship?

2 Kal and I have not been on _____ terms since he started that rumour about me.

3 I didn't mean to _____ our friendship. I wish I could take back the untruthful things I said.

4 My new neighbour is _____ friendly. I think she and I might start hanging out together.

5 Ben and Zac have always gotten on _____. And they seem to do everything together.

6 I'm not one who would ever _____ a secret, but I have to tell you something important.

7 Can I give you some _____ advice? Stay away from Jenn and her friends.

8 Thanks for your honesty. I know it was a hard thing to say, but it's a sign of a(n) _____ friend.

Unit 2
Family

The Ever-changing Family

What constitutes a family has undergone some major shifts over the past few decades. In much of the world there simply is no 'typical' family anymore. 'Different is the new normal', says sociologist Philip Cohen. It's clear today that there are more types of families than ever.

A **nuclear family**, sometimes also known as a **traditional family**, consists of two parents and their children living **under the same roof**. The father is often the **main breadwinner**. This is the idea of family that many people in the industrial word think of. However, in much of the world this type is in decline.

A **single-parent family** consists of one parent with one or more children. A parent may have **gotten divorced**, or they may have **become a widow** or **widower**. In other cases the parent may have never **gotten married** at all. In many parts of the world this type of family is on the rise. This family type has also become more accepted than it was once was.

An **extended family** is the most common type of family in the world. This type includes at least three generations: parents, their grandparents and their children. Other family members such as aunts, uncles and cousins may also live in the same household. In some cases the **family members** choose to live together, and in other cases they share a home out of economic necessity.

A **blended family** is formed when divorced or widowed parents get married for a second time.

Two families merge into one. At least one parent has children who are not **biologically related** to their spouse. This type has become more common over the years. It very often includes **adopted children**.

A childless family is a family where the parents don't have children. The parents either cannot have children or they choose not to **bring children in the world**. For those who choose not to have children, their decision may be due to economic reasons, or just a personal preference.

A community family is not made up of **blood relatives**. It's made up of friends and other people who have filled the role of family members without being related. In this type, you choose your family.

Self-check 1

Complete the descriptions with words from the box. Two words are not used.

adopted	blended	blood	divorced	extended
members	nuclear	related	roof	single

The childless family
The family **1)**_____ in this family includes only the parents.

The 2)_____-parent family
This family type consists of one unmarried parent with one or more children.

The 3)_____ family
There are at least three generations in this family type, all living under the same **4)**_____.

The community family
This family type is made up of people who ae not biologically **5)**_____.

The 6) _____ family
This family type consists of parents and their children.

The 7) _____ family
If a parent with one or more children gets **8)** _____ (or widowed) and then marries someone else, they create this family type.

Self-check 2

Each sentence has an error. Replace the ~~crossed out~~ word.

1 The main ~~relative~~ _____ in my family is my mother. She works outside the home and my father stays home with the kids.

2 My aunt became a ~~divorce~~ _____ after the death of her husband of 30 years. A few years after his death, she chose to marry again.

3 More and more young people are waiting to ~~have~~ _____ married until after they finish their studies.

4 Two parents and their children are known as a ~~blended~~ _____ or nuclear family in many cultures, but that is description may soon change.

5 People often ask me why my partner and I chose not to ~~get~~ _____ children into the world. Why can't people understand that not everyone wants kids?

6 My wife and I have several ~~nuclear~~ _____ children. We couldn't have our own children, so this was a wonderful option for us.

7 We have a huge household. Besides my ~~adopted~~ _____ relatives like my parents and children, it includes my wife's extended family.

Unit 3
Social media

Hannah:	Thanks for accepting my friend request.
Jin-ho:	Oh, sure. I**'m** not that **active on social media**, but I get on sometimes.
Hannah:	I sometimes feel like I**'m addicted to social media**.
Jin-ho:	What do you mean?
Hannah:	I just spend a lot of time online. I'm always checking **trending topics** and **commenting on threads**. I also like to post things.
Jin-ho:	What do you post?
Hannah:	I mostly **post photos**. You know, just pictures of me, of friends, whatever I'm doing.
Jin-ho:	I guess that's what most people use social media for. I don't know. I'm just not that into it. I'm more of a private person I guess.
Hannah:	I can understand that. It's easy to waste time.
Jin-ho:	I did see a funny video the other day. It was of a cat that was jumping rope.
Hannah:	I saw that! It **went viral** and everybody was **sharing the link**.

Trent:	Can you help me with something?
Carmen:	Sure.
Trent:	I'm finally on social media but I'm having some trouble. I know you are on several **social media sites**.
Carmen:	You're on social media? I never thought I'd see the day.
Trent:	Don't laugh! I resisted for a long time, but I'm finally giving in.
Carmen:	Sorry. So what are you trying to do?
Trent:	Well, I **took a selfie** but I can't figure it out how to **upload the photo**.
Carmen:	Oh, that's easy, Just click this … and then this. There.
Trent:	Oh, that *was* easy! And how do I **add friends**?
Carmen:	Look here. These are people you know who already have accounts. Just click this and it will **send a friend request**.
Trent:	How do I **check my messages**?
Carmen:	All your messages are here. See? I'd suggest you go here and **manage your settings**. I'll walk you through it if you like.
Trent:	That would be great.

Self-check 1

Unscramble the words to make sentences. There is one extra word in each set that is not needed.

1 phone / my / with / selfie / took / I / a / made

   _____.

2 your / to / media / messages / check / easy / it's

   _____.

3 addicted / settings / media / is / social / to / Gia

   _____.

4 very / to / social / is / Omar / active / on / media

   _____.

5 settings / viral / you / your / should / manage

   _____.

6 on / never / threads / Emiko / comments / trending

   _____.

Self-check 2

Circle the correct words.

1 A lot of videos go **active / viral**, but then they disappear just as quickly.

2 I rarely **trend / post** photos but my friends and family often tag me in theirs.

3 If I send a friend **request / thread**, how do I know if the person has received it?

4 If you want to **comment / upload** a photo, just make sure that it's not too big.

5 I want to share a **link / media** with you. It's for a job that has recently been advertised.

6 I don't **add / manage** friends very often. I'm already friends with my close friends.

7 How do you decide which social media **site / settings** to join?

8 Understanding **trending / viral** topics on social media is important for internet marketers.

Unit 4
Home

What Is Home?

I've recently graduated from college and have started a new job in a new city. I live in a small, **modest flat**. I don't own it. **I pay rent**. I don't really consider this flat a home, only a place to live for a short time. I've just **put down a deposit** on a **starter home**. I'm going to be a **first-time buyer**! The house is in a **middle-class neighbourhood**, not far from where I work. That will be my home. – *Noirin, 25, Australia*

You can have more than one home. I know someone who still considers their **childhood home** their home. When they **go home** to their parents' house, they say they feel like they **are truly home**. I can see how they would feel that way, especially if they had a happy childhood filled with wonderful memories. But not everyone is so lucky. Some people have lost their homes and are homeless. I wonder how they would answer this question. – *Khalid, 42, Morocco*

I live with my husband and two children in a **single-family home**. This is where we have decided to **put down roots**. It's perfect for our family. It's **in the suburbs**. We have a big kitchen, a living room, a dining room, two bathrooms and three bedrooms. This is our first home, but we hope this will also be our **forever home**. We want to raise our kids here, grow old here, and retire here. I can see lots of grandchildren filling the house in our later years! – *Greta, 28, Germany*

To me home is not about the building. Not everyone has a **home of their own**. Home is where you can feel comfortable, loved and respected. It's where your happiest memories lie. It's where you can dream. It's more about the people and the environment you are in. It's certainly not about a place or having **all the comforts of home**. I guess to me home is an idea, a concept. The saying 'Home is where the heart is' says it all. – *Rafael, 18, Colombia*

Self-check 1

Match the parts. Then use the phrases to complete the sentences.

in	buyer
put down	neighbourhood
home	the suburbs
middle-class	a deposit
first-time	of home
all the comforts	of my own

1   We live in a(n) _____. People of average income can afford to buy here.

2   You don't have to pay for a new home in full, but you need to _____.

3   If you are a(n) _____, it's important that you study the housing market.

4   I live with my family but I'm saving up to buy a(n) _____.

5   Our flat has _____. Our family is very comfortable living there.

6   We're tired of living in the city. We'd like to live _____ someday.

Self-check 2

Circle the correct words.

1   I have a **forever / modest / childhood** flat in the city centre.

2   I don't want to move anymore, It's time for me to **have / pay / put down** roots.

3   I love to visit my **childhood / starter / forever** home. Mom cooks my favourite foods.

4   Is it wasteful to **be / pay / buy** rent, or should I consider buying a home?

5   I thought this was your **truly / forever / comfort** home. Why did you decide to sell it?

6   It's been a very long day, I think I'll **have / go / put down** home soon.

7   We have a(n) **own / suburbs / single-family** home, but we want something bigger.

8   Only when I see my family am I **truly / starter / middle-class** home.

9   This is a great **deposit / starter / childhood** home for a young family.

Unit 5
Academic life

Dong-su:	Are you looking forward to graduation?
Emily:	Of course! My **university life** has been great, but it's time to move onto something else now.
Dong-su:	I heard you were going to **graduate with honours**. That's fantastic!
Emily:	Well, it's been a lot of work.
Dong-su:	What would you say has been the highlight of your college years?
Emily:	Probably the **study abroad program** that I did in Barcelona. That was a great experience.
Dong-su:	What advice would you give new students?
Emily:	**Attend the lectures**! And **hit the books** on weekends. It's best to study at regular times instead of trying to do it all before you **sit for an exam**. I never understand how people can **cram for an exam** and think they'll pass.
Dong-su:	That's good advice. Anything else?
Emily:	Don't feel pressured to **declare a major** right away. Take your time and see what you're interested in. Oh, and one more thing. Have fun! Your university experience should be much more than just classes and marks.

Lori:	Alex, I haven't seen you in ages. How was your trip?
Alex:	Oh, it was great. I've only recently gotten back.
Lori:	You were in Australia, right?
Alex:	Yeah. I travelled around there, but also worked in New Zealand for a while.
Lori:	And now what? Are you planning on going to college this year?
Alex:	I am. I'm really glad I **took a gap year**, but now I'm ready to start school.
Lori:	Are you still thinking about Barton University?
Alex:	No, I've decided to go to a **two-year college**. I **received a scholarship** from them, which is a huge help.
Lori:	Congratulations!
Alex:	Thanks, but it will only cover the **tuition fees**. I still need to pay for my accommodation.
Lori:	Will you need to **take out a student loan**?
Alex:	I hope not. A friend of mine had to borrow money, and is still trying to **pay off the loan**. I don't want to be in debt when I graduate.
Lori:	Are you planning to **live off campus**?
Alex:	No, I'm going to **live in the halls of residence**. I can save money and meet people that way. Maybe I'll get my own place after a semester or two.

Self-check 1

Circle the correct words.

1 I am going to go to a two-year **graduate / college / honours**.

2 Do you planning to live **of / off / to** campus?

3 What study abroad **major / program / tuition** are you considering?

4 Do you think it's helpful to cram **on / off / for** an exam?

5 I hope I **receive / take / take out** a scholarship. Otherwise I can't afford college.

6 The tuition **loans / degrees / fees** at that private school are crazy!

7 My **graduation / major / university** life has been filled with many late nights at the library.

8 If I take **out / up / off** a student loan, when do I have to pay the money back?

Self-check 2

Complete the descriptions with words from the box. Two words are not used.

attend	cram for	declare	graduate	hit
live	pay off	sit for	take	take out

1 If you want to do well in college, you have to _____ the lectures.

2 I'm planning to _____ in the halls of residence during my first year.

3 I have a big exam next week. I really need to _____ the books this weekend.

4 Try to _____ your student loan as soon as you can. It's not good to be in debt.

5 I heard you were going to _____ with honours. Your parents must be very proud.

6 I know it's hard to choose, but you have to _____ a major at some point.

7 More and more people are choosing to _____ a gap year to travel or work.

8 When you _____ an exam, make sure you are well-prepared and well-rested.

Unit 6
Food

Healthy Eating at University

Some students who come to university have to rely on feeding themselves for the first time. A lot happens during those first few weeks, and developing **good eating habits** may not be your top priority. You don't need to survive on **fast food**. There is no reason why you can't have a healthy, **balanced diet** if you follow these eight tips.

1. Make a list
    Always try to **make a shopping list** and get what you need for the week ahead. Also, never **shop on an empty stomach**.

2. Buy fresh
    Try not to buy too much **packaged food**. These items will probably be high in salt and fat. If you do, be sure to **check the ingredients** carefully.

3. Avoid sugary snacks
    We all need to **satisfy our sweet tooth** from time to time, but avoid filling up your shopping cart with **junk food** like biscuits and chocolate.

4. Snack smart

It's easy to **work up an appetite** after a long day on campus. And it's OK to snack. Just eat the right things, like fruit and nuts.

5. Skip **ready-made meals**

You may be tempted to pick up meals you can simply heat up and eat. But try to **cook from scratch**. It takes more time, but it's healthier, and it will save you money.

6. Have a few **go-to recipes**

It's fine to cook some of your favourites again and again. You are at university to study after all. An easy stir-fry or a quick pasta sauce can go a long way.

7. Consider a slow cooker

A slow cooker can be your best friend. Toss in the ingredients for soup or curry in the morning and you have a **home-cooked meal** waiting for you when you get back from class. Make extra and freeze for later to save even more time.

8. Eat certain foods in moderation

When you are out and want to **grab a bite to eat**, choose carefully. Pizza is fine as a **quick snack** sometimes, but eating it too often may not be good for your waistline.

Self-check 1

Circle the correct word. Then use the phrases to complete the sentences.

check / grab / make	a bite to eat
do / work / make	a shopping list
make / check / have	a balanced diet
balance / shop / work up	an appetite
shop on / eat / develop	an empty stomach
develop / work / do	good eating habits
make / have / satisfy	your sweet tooth
cook **to / from / a**	scratch

1   We all need to _____. Then we have them our entire lives.

2   All this work really caused me to _____. I'm so hungry now!

3   Think about what you need before you go to the market. Then _____.

4   I skipped lunch, so can we _____ somewhere near here?

5   If you need to _____, this bakery sells excellent cakes.

6   Ken doesn't _____. He eats junk food all the time.

7   It's not good to _____. You make poor choices when you're hungry.

8   Why not try to _____ more? Tinned soup is high in salt and you have all the ingredients for soup here.

Self-check 2

Circle the correct words.

1   I sometimes have a **quick / fast / junk** snack before I head home from class.

2   How often do you eat **go-to / fast / balanced** food, like pizza and burgers?

3   It's smart to **make / shop / check** the ingredients before you buy anything.

4   When I visit my parents, I always enjoy a **recipe / home-cooked / scratch** meal.

5   I avoid eating **junk / bite / balanced** food like crisps and chips.

6   I have one **ready-made / scratch / go-to** recipe I often make when people drop by.

7   I avoid buying **quick / packaged / habit** food because I prefer making my own meals.

8   I like **ready-made / go-to / junk** meals because I can just heat them up in the microwave.

Unit 7
Appearance

Amanda:	Thanks for agreeing to pick up my mother from the airport.
Haley:	That's OK. I'm glad I can help.
Amanda:	I didn't realise I had a meeting at that time, so I really appreciate you doing this.
Haley:	You know, I've never met your mother. What does she look like?
Amanda:	Oh, well, she's not very tall. She **has a slim figure**. And she **has red hair**.
Haley:	Is her hair long or short?
Amanda:	I'd say she **has shoulder-length hair**.
Haley:	How old is she?
Amanda:	She's 55, but she **looks young for her age**. Most everyone says she **has a youthful appearance**.
Haley:	OK.
Amanda:	And she**'s** always **fashionably dressed**. She'll probably be wearing a nice jacket. Hang on. You know what would be easier?
Haley:	What?
Amanda:	Why don't I just pull up a photo of her from my phone?

Andy:	Grandpa, is this a photo of you?
Grandpa:	Let's see … yes, a very old photo of me.
Andy:	I've never seen this before. How old are you here?
Grandpa:	I think I**'m in my early 20s**.
Andy:	Is that your army uniform?
Grandpa:	Yes, so this would have been while I was still in the army. I **had a full head of hair** back then. Now I**'m going bald**.
Andy:	Oh, come on. I think you are **growing old gracefully**.
Grandpa:	Well, you're kind to say so.
Andy:	You **have** such **an athletic build** here. Look at your **broad shoulders**.
Grandpa:	Well, I admit I **was in good shape** then.
Andy:	You **strongly resemble** Dad here.
Grandpa:	You think so?
Andy:	Definitely. You **have the same eyes**.

English Collocations in Context

Self-check 1

Circle the correct word. Then use the phrases to complete the sentences.

is / has	red hair
is / has	fashionably dressed
is / has	in his early 20s
is / has	the same eyes
is / has	in good shape
is / has	shoulder-length hair
is / has	a full head of hair

1 My daughter _____ as me, but hers are dark green. Mine are light green.

2 Julie's hair used to be long, but she trimmed it. Now she _____.

3 Craig looks about 15 but he _____. He wishes he looked older.

4 Michael _____, but he wants to dye it a dark brown. I hope he doesn't.

5 Chen was overweight last year but he joined a gym and now _____ again.

6 Patricia _____ whenever she goes out. She spends a lot on clothes.

7 Our baby is only one month old and oddly he already _____.
   We may need to cut it.

Self-check 2

Complete the sentences with words from the box. Two words are not used.

athletic   bald   broad   fashionably   old   same   slim
strongly   young   youthful

1 Annette has a _____ figure, but she says she can eat whatever she wants.

2 My uncle is 58 but he has a(n) _____ appearance. Some think he's in his 40s.

3 Penny is 54 but looks _____ for her age. People think she's around 40.

4 Jeff is only 30 but he's already going _____. That's why he started wearing caps.

5 Daniel works as a construction workers. Is that why he has such _____ shoulders?

6 Jo _____ resembles her sister even though there's a six-year age difference.

7 Raul has a(n) _____ build, but strangely he says he rarely participates in any sports.

8 Why do people get cosmetic surgery? It's better to just grow _____ gracefully.

Unit 8
Travel

The Art of Travel Planning

Have you ever been overwhelmed by the idea of **planning a trip**? There is a lot to think about. Where should I go? What kind of trip interests me? What documents do I need? Planning needn't be a stressful experience.

First, consider your budget. Look at your finances and figure out how much you want to spend. Knowing your exact budget will help you focus your trip and make other decisions that much easier.

Next, decide who you will travel with. Do you like traveling with others, or do you prefer to **travel solo** so you can **travel at your own pace**? Traveling with a large group is not for everyone.

Then think about the type of trip that's right for you. There are many options. Do you want a **self-catering holiday**, or perhaps an **all-inclusive resort** better suits you? Do you want to **take a road trip** and **take in the sights** in your own country, or do you want to **go abroad** to somewhere exotic or **off the beaten track**?

You are now ready to choose your actual destination. You might get inspiration from the internet, from other people or from brochures. There is a lot of information out there, and for some, actually choosing the destination can be the hardest part of travel planning.

After you decide the where, then focus on the when and the how long. Some people love to **travel off season** when prices are lower and there are fewer crowds. Others may not have the luxury of choosing when they travel.

There is still a lot do. What transport will you use? You may need to **book a flight** or **reserve a train ticket**. Spend time online looking at hotels or other accommodation as this will likely be one of your biggest expenses You can often **score a deal** with just a little effort.

Finally, be sure to check if you need to **obtain a visa** for any country you will visit. If you do, see if you can get it online, or if the country has a **visa on arrival**. And of course make sure your passport has not expired!

Self-check 1

Circle the correct word. Then use the phrases to complete the sentences.

score	**on arrival / a deal / the sights**
take in	**a flight / a tour / the sights**
travel	**off season / a visa / a road trip**
go	**a trip / abroad / a deal**
book	**a visa / a flight / off the beaten track**
obtain	**solo / travel / a visa**
plan	**a trip / solo / a train ticket**

1 Everyone goes to Greece in summer. I prefer to _____, in May or October.

2 I can't _____ because I haven't got a passport, so I'll stay close to home.

3 I was able to _____ on my ticket to Mexico City. I saved 40%!

4 Any travel agent can help you _____ that is affordable and personal.

5 After I get to a new city, I like to walk around and _____ at my own pace.

6 I need to _____ soon before the air fares go up. What airline should I fly?

7 To _____ for Russia, send your passport to their embassy and then pay the fee.

Self-check 2

Each sentence has an error. Replace the ~~crossed out~~ word.

1 A self-catering ~~travel~~ _____ gives you the flexibility to cook for yourself.

2 I would love to get in the car and ~~drive~~ _____ a road trip somewhere.

3 I avoid tourists traps, and much prefer to travel off the beaten ~~tour~~ _____.

4 This is a popular line with tourists, so I suggest you ~~plan~~ _____ a train ticket in advance.

5 I don't mind traveling with others, but I sometimes prefer to ~~book~~ _____ solo.

6 You can get a visa ~~by~~ _____ arrival. You don't need to obtain one in advance.

7 This all-~~group~~ _____ resort includes your hotel and your food, drinks and activities.

8 I like to travel ~~with~~ _____ my pace. That's why I avoid bus tours and other group travel.

Unit 9
Leisure

Zara: How's school?

Marcus: Exhausting! No, actually, everything is going great.

Zara: You study full-time, but you also work part-time, don't you?

Marcus: Yes.

Zara: What do you **do for fun**?

Marcus: Oh, I mainly just like to **hang out with friends**. We often **get together over a coffee** and just talk.

Zara: What do you talk about?

Marcus: Everything – school, family, relationships, what movies are playing. You name it.

Zara: Have you seen any movies lately?

Marcus: Yeah, I **streamed a movie** last night in fact. It was one of the Star Wars movie.

Zara: What did you think?

Marcus: I **thoroughly enjoyed** it.

Zara: So, you have any time now?

Marcus: Sure. What do you have in mind?

Zara: How about we **grab some lunch**?

Marcus: Sounds great!

Jerome: What are you doing this summer? Do you have plans?

Lydia: I do. I'm going to work as a camp counsellor.

Jerome: Really? I never went to summer camp. I want to, but never had the chance. So what does your job entail?

Lydia: Well, I did it last year as well. I mostly supervised different activities with the kids.

Jerome: Like what?

Lydia: We **went swimming** on most days. On some days we'd **go for a hike**. Lots of stuff.

Jerome: Did you play sports?

Lydia: Sure. We **played football** a lot! Then at night we'd often **have a cookout** and sit around the campfire. I heard a lot of ghost stories! The kids **totally get into** it.

Jerome: I suppose you want good weather at a summer camp.

Lydia: Yes, but it isn't all about **outdoor activities**. At night we might **do a puzzle.** The main thing is we want the kids to **develop an interest** in something. It can be sports, or arts and crafts, or even a musical instrument. They are there to **have fun**.

Self-check 1

Complete the sentences with words from the box. Three words are not used.

become	develop	do	go	go for	
grab	hang out	know	stream	tell	

1   When it's cold out I like stay inside and _____ a puzzle.

2   The lake is still a little chilly, but let's _____ swimming anyway.

3   How about we _____ some lunch? I haven't eaten anything today.

4   Do you want to _____ a hike? There are some nice trails around here.

5   On weekends I usually _____ with friends. It's the only time we can catch up.

6   I'm not very good, but I have started to _____ an interest in painting.

7   There's no cinema around here. Why don't we stay in and _____ a movie?

Self-check 2

Circle the correct words.

Summer Language Camp

What do you do for **1) leisure / fun / interest** in summer? Why not join our one-week summer language camp. We have a wide range of **2) out / outdoor / together** activities available, and you do everything in English! In the morning you have a wide choice of fun activities to try: swimming, hiking, **3) doing / playing / going** football, cooking, playing games, or doing arts and crafts. The only requirement is that you **4) have / do / enjoy** fun. In the afternoon you **5) make / do / get** together over a coffee and practise your English together in a relaxing setting with any of our language volunteers. At night we **6) have / take / make** a cookout where we sit around the campfire chatting and telling stories. Everyone totally **7) has / goes / gets** into it, and they soon forget they are doing it all in English. Past participants **8) markedly / thoroughly / funnily** enjoyed their time with us. Visit our website to read their reviews and testimonials.

Unit 10
Shopping

Black Friday

The American holiday of Thanksgiving occurs on the fourth Thursday of November. The day after Thanksgiving is known as Black Friday. It is a day full of sales and **shopping deals**. It's considered the beginning of the unofficial **holiday shopping season** in the United States. Some believe it's called Black Friday because it's the day when stores go from losing money to finally **being in the black**. It's a day when many people **go on a shopping spree**, spending a lot of money in the process.

The idea of retailers offering big savings the day after Thanksgiving started long before it was ever called Black Friday. Many employers gave their employees the Friday after Thanksgiving off so their employees had a four-day weekend. People used the time to get a head start on their Christmas shopping.

Today, retailers **attract customers** by offering promotions and **substantial discounts** on electronics, toys, clothes and other items. They open their doors during the pre-dawn hours and extend their store hours until midnight. Some retailers stay open for the entire Thanksgiving holiday weekend. Stores almost always enjoy a huge **spike in sales**.

Avid **bargain-hunters** sometimes camp out overnight on Thanksgiving to secure a place in the queue at their favourite store. Some **die-hard shoppers** skip Thanksgiving altogether and camp out days before to **pick up a bargain**.

Retailers can spend months planning their Black Friday sales. They use this day as an opportunity to offer **rock-bottom prices** on inventory that is overstocked or difficult to sell otherwise. They often **slash prices** on big-ticket items and **top-selling brands** of TVs, smart devices, and other electronic goods. Their strategy is to get customers into the stores with these items, but then sell other items as well that provide higher profits.

Black Friday has been known to lead to arguments, fights, and even serious violence. When an in-demand item **hits the shops**, it can lead people to act poorly. Tragically, in 2008 a shopper at a **big-box store** was killed when he was pushed over and trampled to death by over-eager shoppers after the doors were opened.

For online retailers, a similar tradition has arisen on the Monday following Thanksgiving. Known as Cyber Monday, it's the unofficial start of the online holiday shopping season. In terms of sales, it's proven wildly successful, even overtaking sales from Back Friday. In 2018, Cyber Monday sales in the US were nearly $8 billion. Black Friday's sales were just $6 billion.

English Collocations in Context

Self-check 1

Match the parts. Then use the phrases to complete the definitions.

is	prices
hits	customers
slashes	on a shopping spree
goes	in the black
picks up	the shops
attracts	a bargain

1 When a store _____ it lowers what the customer pays.

2 If a shop _____, they bring more people in to shop.

3 If a company _____, it's making a profit.

4 When an item _____, it becomes available for purchase.

5 Someone _____ when they get an item at a much lower price.

6 When someone _____, they buy a lot of things in a short time.

Self-check 2

Circle the correct words.

1 I like shopping in smaller shops. A big-box **store / sale / price** can feel so impersonal.

2 Now is the time to get a new TV. That shop is offering rock-**low / -down / -bottom** prices.

3 Many retailers enjoy a spike **of / at / in** sales at the end of the year.

4 There were **shop- / bargain- / money**-hunters waiting at the doors at 7:00 am.

5 I check several web sites before I buy to find the best **shopping / spree / bargain** deals.

6 This is the **high- / top- / one**-selling brand of ramen, but I don't care for it.

7 Several shops are offering substantial **discounts / prices / seasons** on last-year's TVs.

8 The holiday shopping **store / price / season** seems to start earlier and earlier every year.

9 To find the best deals, die-**hard / -tough / -black** shoppers compare prices.

Unit 11
Abilities

Sasha:	That meal was fantastic.
Adam:	I'm glad you enjoyed it.
Sasha:	You are very talented.
Adam:	Thanks, but I'm not so sure. At least not in cooking.
Sasha:	No? Well, what do you think you're **good at**?
Adam:	Let's see … I suppose art. I can paint pretty well.
Sasha:	And your drawings are great.
Adam:	I appreciate that. You know, some people say I'**m a natural**. Who knows if it's true, but it's a nice thing to hear.
Sasha:	It's true. What about **athletic ability**? Are you good at sports?
Adam:	Not at all. Sports **are not my strong suit**.
Sasha:	I hear you. I have a complete **lack of skills** in sports of any kind.
Adam:	You **have the ability to** add numbers in your head very easily. I've seen you.
Sasha:	That true. I do **possess skills** in maths.
Adam:	And that's a very **practical skill** to have.

Matt:	Listen to this violinist. She's so talented.
Sun-hee:	She is.
Matt:	Did you know she's only 8 years old.
Sun-hee:	Really? That's amazing.
Matt:	Do you think some people are naturally good at certain things?
Sun-hee:	That's a tough one. I think it's probably true for some people. I do know that some people seem to **have an ear for music**, for example.
Matt:	This young girl probably does.
Sun-hee:	I've heard of people who can perform a song immediately after hearing it.
Matt:	So you believe that some people **are born with talent**?
Sun-hee:	I guess I do. I know it's true with some athletes. They clearly show **raw talent** from an early age.
Matt:	Any examples?
Sun-hee:	How about Lionel Messi? He's been described as **a born footballer**. He **had a natural talent for** it from an early age. But I know other people **acquire skills through** lots of practice. I've read that it takes 10,000 hours of practice to **gain mastery** in something. Practice makes perfect after all!
Matt:	I've heard that too, but I know not everyone agrees.

Self-check 1

Circle the correct words.

1 Mozart had a **master / natural / skill** talent for music from a very early age.

2 She is good **on / to / at** fixing computers because she went to a trade school.

3 Ahmed is a **skill / born / talent** artist. Art is what he was destined to do.

4 I'm not just bad at dancing. I have a complete **lack / none / bad** of skills!

5 Caroline has an ear **by / to / for** music. She doesn't even need to read the music.

6 I wouldn't say I was born **to / in / with** talent. I became good at chess by practising.

7 It takes time to gain **master / mastery / mastering** in the piano.

8 Unfortunately, they don't really have much **talent / skill / athletic** ability.

Self-check 2

Unscramble the words to make sentences.

1 a / he / natural / is

   _____.

2 skills / possesses / she / business / in

   _____.

3 skills / he / practice / acquires / through

   _____.

4 practical / is / driving / skill / a / very

   _____.

5 in / demonstrate / they / raw / talent / tennis

   _____.

6 ability / she / do / job / the / the / to / has

   _____.

7 his / not / languages / are / suit / strong

   _____.

Unit 12
Weather

Weather in the UK

Weather affects us all. **Gorgeous weather** makes us happy, and **gloomy weather** can put us in a bad mood. People usually have something to say about the weather. Talking about it is a typical conversation starter, and there can be strong opinions shared about the weather. This is true in many countries, including the UK.

The UK has very **changeable weather**. This means that it can change from one day to the next. or even within a day. **Fine weather** in the morning can suddenly turn nasty in the afternoon. Britons are used to this, and take such changes in weather in stride.

The weather across the UK can vary greatly. There can **be not a cloud in the sky** in the south, while the north will **be under a blanket of snow**. But the UK generally does not experience **extreme weather**. One season gradually turns to the next.

The Atlantic Ocean warms the isles in summer. July and August are the hottest months. While they are hot, they are not too hot. It's rare to **have a heatwave**, though they do happen. Winters can be cold, but are rarely **bitterly cold**. Much of this is due to the effects of the Atlantic Ocean. It helps to keep the country mild in winter.

There can be **gentle winds**, or they can be quite strong. It all depends where they are, They tend to come from the southwest, and are strongest on the Atlantic coastline.

There is often **bright sunshine** in May and June. **Clear blue skies** are the norm on most days in the south of the country. But the UK has a reputation for being rainy and overcast. Rainfall varies across the isles, with more rain occurring in the west and at higher elevations. There are bouts of **pouring rain**, but it's more likely there will just be a **light drizzle**. The wettest months are in winter.

The UK, especially London, is also famous for its fog. It's more common inland than along the coasts, and tends to occur more in autumn and winter. Fog can cause a lot of problems, and contributes to traffic accidents and airport delays.

So if you're planning a trip to the UK, it's always wise to check the **weather forecast**.

Self-check 1

Complete the sentences with words from the box. Two words are not used.

blue	bright	changeable	cold	fine
heat	pouring	snow	weather	wind

1 The announcer said we should expect five days of clear _____ skies.

2 The _____ forecast for today calls for high temperatures along the coast.

3 We had to stay inside all day because of the _____ rain.

4 The _____ sunshine made it a perfect day for an afternoon picnic.

5 We enjoyed a week of _____ weather on our holiday. We sunbathed every day.

6 The snowstorm caused the entire country to be bitterly _____.

7 California can have _____ weather because it can be hot one minute and cold the next.

8 The _____ wave lasted for a week until a cold front caused the temperature to drop.

Self-check 2

Each sentence has an error. Replace the crossed out word.

1 We had such gorgeous ~~season~~ _____ on our trip to Thailand. It's the rainy season right now, so we were lucky.

2 I don't think you really need to take your umbrella today. The weather forecast says we're probably only going to get a ~~soft~~ _____ drizzle

3 Our holiday in Ecuador was very special. It was a beautiful sight to see the Andes ~~on~~ _____ a blanket of snow.

4 We've had ~~gloom~~ _____ weather for a week now. It's been overcast with no sign of the sun.

5 I'll never forget our trip across the Australian Outback. We drove for hours and there was not a ~~sunshine~~ _____ in the sky.

6 Many countries around the world suffer from ~~extremely~~ _____ weather. Blizzards, hurricanes and dust storms can cause extensive damage.

7 One of the best things about our trip was sitting on the beach enjoying the ~~tender~~ _____ winds.

Unit 13
Personality

Giovanni:	Can I ask for some advice? I was paired up with two classmates to work on a project together. This project will be a big part of our final mark, so I want to do well on it.
Mariko:	So what's the problem?
Giovanni:	Well, one person **has a dominant personality**. She's very **strong-willed** and wants to have the final say in every decision.
Mariko:	Is she **closed-minded**?
Giovanni:	Yeah. She thinks everything should be her way, or no way.
Mariko:	She doesn't sound like a team player.
Giovanni:	She's not at all. She's **quick-tempered** as well. She gets angry if she thinks we aren't prepared for something.
Mariko:	That's tough. What about the other person on the team?
Giovanni:	It's just the opposite. He's so **easy-going**, and he's really **soft-spoken**. He doesn't contribute much to our discussions.
Mariko:	Why not?
Giovanni:	I think he's just **painfully shy**. It's unfortunate because he has good ideas.
Mariko:	OK, well, here's what I would do ...

Interviewer:	I appreciate you coming in for this interview today, Ms Silva.
Ms Silva:	Thank you.
Interviewer:	Can you tell a bit about yourself? And what makes you a good fit for this position?
Ms Silva:	Well, I've been working as a data analyst for a few year now. I've always been good with numbers and figures. People say I'**m a numbers person.**
Interviewer:	Are you comfortable working with others?
Ms Silva:	Oh, of course. I'm definitely a team player. My team members have told me that I **have an analytical mind** that helps me in my decision-making.
Interviewer:	So why would you want to leave your current position?
Ms Silva:	I'm ready to move onto the next challenge. Your company has a great reputation for innovation, and I'd like to be part of your company's growth.

Interviewer:	What **character traits** do you possess that would serve you well in this role?
Ms Silva:	I've been described as **well-organised** and **hard-working** by my current boss.
Interviewer:	That's good to hear. We definitely need someone who is **self-reliant**. We want someone who can hit the ground running from day one.
Ms Silva:	That's me. I also **have a positive attitude**. That may be my greatest strength.
Interviewer:	OK. What would you say is your greatest weakness?
Ms Silva:	Hmm, well, I suppose I can be **overly cautious** at times. But that may not be a bad thing. Not everything comes down to numbers. There are many other factors in any decision.

Self-check 1

Match the parts. Then use the phrases to complete the definitions.

quick-	reliant
closed-	going
strong-	spoken
hard-	working
soft-	willed
self-	minded
easy-	tempered

1 _____ = said in a quiet voice

2 _____ = easily made angry

3 _____ = relaxed and casual in style

4 _____ = very determined to do something

5 _____ = not willing to consider other's ideas

6 _____ = putting a lot of effort into one's work

7 _____ = able to make decisions by oneself

Self-check 2

Complete the descriptions with words from the box. Two words are not used.

> attitude   dominant   numbers   mind   organised
>
> overly   soft   shy   traits   working

1   Kara has several character _____ that I admire. She always helps other people and she's not afraid to admit when she needs help herself.

2   Andrew is painfully _____. He never raises his hand in class to ask questions and is very quiet in small-group discussions.

3   Rachel is a(n) _____ person. She seems very comfortable making annual sales projections.

4   Lucinda has a(n) _____ personality that can come across as pushy if you don't know her well.

5   When he first started his business, people said that Chen was _____ cautious. He said it was all part of his three-year business plan.

6   Kelsey is known for having an analytical _____. She uses knowledge, facts and information to make decisions.

7   Justin is not well-_____ at all. His desk is always a mess and when you ask him for something it take a long time for him to find it.

8   Svetlana has a positive _____ when it comes to her job. She doesn't make much money, but she's always smiling and doing her best.

Unit 14
Nature

Seven Natural Wonders of the World

1. **Victoria Falls**

   Victoria Falls is located on the border of Zambia and Zimbabwe. The falls measure over 1.7 kilometers across and over 100 metres high. Over 500 million litres of **water cascades** over the falls every minute. The area around the falls is rich in **flora and fauna**.

2. **Harbour of Rio de Janeiro**

   The **natural harbour** in Rio de Janeiro, Brazil, is the gorgeous sight. The **lush rainforest** around the harbour has several iconic mountains, including Corcovado Peak and Sugar Loaf. An important waterway for shipping, huge ships can often be seen in the harbour.

3. **Mount Everest**

   Mount Everest, a peak in the Himalayan **mountain range** between Nepal and China, is the world's tallest mountain. It's extremely dangerous to **climb the mountain**. Over the years hundreds have died trying to **reach the summit**.

4. **Grand Canyon**

   At more than 1.6 km deep and between 6 and 30 km wide, the Grand Canyon in the US is one of the largest canyons in the world. This **natural wonder** was formed through erosion between 30 and 70 million years old. What one sees as a **barren landscape** from the top changes quickly into a land of waterfalls below the rim.

5. **Great Barrier Reef**

   The Great Barrier Reef is the world's largest living structure, stretching over 1,600 km along the east coast of Australia. It consists of more than 2,500 individual reefs and 900 islands. The reef is rich in **marine life**. More than 1,500 species of fish call the coral **reef system** home.

6. **Paricutin Volcano**

   Mexico's Paricutin Volcano is the youngest volcano in the world. Although the **sparsely populated** area around Paricutin remains **volcanically active**, it is now a **dormant volcano**. Visitors can view Parícutin from its base or from its crater.

7. **Northern Lights**

   The Northern Lights are a unique and enchanting **natural phenomenon**. Often greenish or reddish in colour, these dancing lights are caused by the emission of particles of light by electrons in the atmosphere.

Self-check 1

Complete the email with words from the box. Two words are not used.

> cascade   landscape   life   population   rainforest
>
> range   reach   system   volcano   wonder

Hi Mark,

Thanks for your email. I'm glad you are interested in visiting Indonesia. We had a great time there earlier this year, and here is what I recommend.

On Sumatra we visited several national parks. We had hoped to see wild orangutans, but we never did. It was hard to walk through the lush 1)_____, but our fun guide helped us. Near Lake Toba we visited Sipiso Pisa Waterfall. It was a long, hot walk to the bottom – 700 steps, but worth it. To hear the 2) water _____ all around you is something you'll never forget.

On Java we saw the sunrise from Mount Bromo. It's part of the Tengger mountain 3)_____. Bromo is not a dormant 4)_____ – it's active! But we felt safe. There is a barren 5)_____ around the volcano, but it's so beautiful. It really is a natural 6)_____ that should be on everyone's bucket list.

We ended our trip in Bali. It was touristy but we enjoyed it, especially walking in the gorgeous rice fields. One day we tried to go snorkeling. Sadly, the reef 7)_____ where we were was not so healthy, but we managed to see some marine 8)_____ – mostly fish.

All for now,
Jess

Self-check 2

Circle the correct words.

1   Mongolia is one of the most sparsely **lived / populous / populated** countries in Asia.

2   It took us five days to **range / reach / grasp** the summit of Mt Kilimanjaro.

3   Dubai's Jebel Ali doesn't have a **nature / natural / naturalist** harbour. It was artificially made.

4   Kilauea in Hawaii has been volcanically **active / effective / busy** for many years.

5   Much of the flora and **plants / habitat / fauna** in the Amazon has not been recorded yet.

6   If you want to **rise / climb / soar** the mountain, you'd better start training.

7   A tornado is a **honest / true / natural** phenomenon that is fascinating to see, but often deadly.

Unit 15
Routines

Julio:	What's a **typical day** like for you?
Megan:	What do you mean?
Julio:	I mean do you have a **daily routine**?
Megan:	Oh, sure. During the week I generally I like to **get an early start** to the day.
Julio:	How early?
Megan:	I get up around 6:30. I **clean my teeth**, stretch for a few minutes, and then **take a shower**.
Julio:	And after that?
Megan:	Well, I **get dressed** and **do my makeup**.
Julio:	Do you have breakfast at home?
Megan:	No. I usually just eat something at my desk after I get to work.
Julio:	Why is that?
Megan:	Well, I'm not really hungry until then. I just get a quick muffin or a bagel.
Julio:	What do you do in the evening? Do you cook at home?
Megan:	Well, I'm usually too tired after work, so I usually just **order takeaway** for dinner.

Elena::	What do you usually do on weekends?
Noah:	Well, I'm not really **a morning person**, so I usually like to sleep in on Saturdays.
Elena:	That sounds nice.
Noah:	Yeah, it is. After I get up, I **do chores** around the house. I don't really have time for them during the week.
Elena:	What kind of chores?
Noah:	Oh, I **do the laundry**, and **take out the rubbish** – lots of things. It's not the most exciting Saturday morning.
Elena:	Do you then have the afternoon for yourself?
Noah:	Not really. In the afternoon I usually have to **run errands** around town. I go to the bank, the supermarket, the post office – there are always **a million and one things to do**.
Elena:	Do you **take a nap** in the afternoon?
Noah:	Sometimes, if I have time.
Elena:	After all that, you probably go out on Saturday night, right?
Noah:	Hardly. At night I just want to **curl up with a good book** and read.

Self-check 1

Unscramble the words to make sentences.

1 I / morning / a / am / person / not

_____.

2 boring / routine / daily / very / is / my

_____.

3 start / get / to / an / like / early / I

_____.

4 I / a / typical / have / day / don't

_____.

5 he / out / take / to / rubbish / hates / the

_____.

6 in / her / minutes / makeup / she / five / does

_____.

7 with / I / curling / up / a / book / enjoy / good

_____.

8 things / a / do / to / and / one / there / are / million

_____.

Self-check 2

Complete the sentences with words from the box. Two words are not used.

chores	dressed	errands	laundry	makeup
nap	routine	shower	takeaway	teeth

1 I usually do _____ such as cleaning on Saturday afternoon.

2 I take a _____ because my flat doesn't have a bathtub.

3 If I'm tired in the afternoon I sometimes take a _____ at my desk.

4 All my clothes are dirty so it's time to do the _____.

5   I wish I had an hour off work so I could run _____.

6   I clean my _____ three times a day, or after every meal.

7   It takes me a long time to get _____ because I can never decide what to wear.

8   I'm too tired to cook. Let's order _____ from the new Lebanese place.

Unit 16
Work

Dying Jobs

In this week's blog, I want to talk about jobs. Do you know anyone who **makes a living** as a bowling pin setter? I certainly don't. That job died out long ago. There are many examples of dead jobs as well as jobs that are slowly dying. One is the postal worker. We have postal workers today, but their **job prospects** for the future are poor. The reason? Technology.

Technology is also killing fast-food cooks. Even though this is already often **unskilled work** with low pay, big chain restaurants are finding it cheaper to prepare food off-site and simply have employees reheat it. Also, travel agents might want to **apply for a job** in a different field. It's easier than ever to book flights, hotels and tours online.

Would you like to be a newspaper reporter? There are newspaper reporters, but it's seen more and more as a **dead-end job**. You might want to **look for a job** as a reporter for a website or video channel instead of a print newspaper.

Another dying job is the door-to-door salesperson. Many people now shop online. It's easy, fast and you can take your time. If someone in your family is a door-to-door salesperson, you may not want to **follow in their footsteps**.

Finally, there's the computer operator. This **nine-to-five job** was once considered a **decent job**, but not these days. Most people now have personal computers with excellent software, so many computer operators are **being made redundant**. They may want to **make a career move** before this happens.

But all is not lost. There are many newer jobs that did not exist a generation ago. All exist now because of changing technology. One of the fastest growing jobs today is app developer. An **entry-level position** as a developer is not too hard to find.

Blogging is not so new, but blogging as a job is. Many companies now pay bloggers to write about their products. Bloggers have **flexible hours**, which suits many people. They also **work from home**, which saves companies money.

Another job that didn't exist in the past is social media manager. This person suggests ways a company can use all of the types of social media out there.

This brings me to the job of chief listening officer. You read that right – chief listening officer. What do they do? Their **day-to-day work** involves listening to conversations and seeing what people are discussing online. They want to see what customers are saying about the company.

Will these hot jobs be dying jobs a generation from now? Probably not, but what jobs will exist? No one knows. We'll have to wait and see.

Self-check 1

Circle the correct words.

Lucy:	How's the job?
Khadija:	It's OK, but I think I may 1) **work / make / look for** a career move soon.
Lucy:	Really? Why is that?
Khadija:	I don't think the job 2) **work / careers / prospects** here are that great.
Lucy:	In what way?
Khadija:	I just don't see myself getting a promotion anytime soon. To be honest, it's kind of a dull 3) **nine-and-five / nine until five / nine-to-five** job that doesn't really challenge me. The 4) **day-of-day / day-to-day / days and days** work has become kind of tedious.
Lucy:	So what are you thinking of doing?
Khadija:	I may 5) **make / follow / apply for** a job with a start-up company. A friend of mine from college started a small company last year and she's looking for several people. It would be an entry-level 6) **position / work / career**, but I'd be able to work 7) **by / from / to** home, which is appealing. I'd also have 8) **change / flexible / day-to-day** hours.
Lucy:	I would enjoy that. Well, let me know what you decide to do.

Self-check 2

Each sentence has an error. Replace the ~~crossed out~~ word.

1   This really is a dead-end ~~work~~ _____. I will probably be doing the exact same thing a year from now that I'm doing today.

2   Some examples of unskilled ~~career~~ _____ includes washing dishes and serving coffee. These types of jobs don't tend to pay very well.

3   I was told I was being made ~~fired~~ _____ as they company could no longer afford to pay my salary.

4   Ken makes a ~~job~~ _____ by taking on seasonal construction jobs, but he often complains about not having job security.

5   Don't rush the job search after you graduate. It can take some time to find a decent ~~experience~~ _____.

6   When you look for a ~~work~~ _____, you may want to consider a headhunter. This person can directly put you in touch with potential employers.

7   My father was a doctor and has always wanted me to ~~go~~ _____ in his footsteps. He was disappointed that I chose to be an artist.

Unit 17
Sleep

Aria:	I think we've made good progress on the Wilson report
Lukas:	So do I.
Aria:	Oh, good. Do you think we can take a short break?
Lukas:	Of course. Is everything OK?
Aria:	Yeah, I'm just tired.
Lukas:	Late night?
Aria:	No, I did**n't get a wink of sleep** last night. I just **tossed and turned** the whole night.
Lukas:	You got no sleep at all? Well, you do look sleepy.
Aria:	Honestly, I pretty much **feel dead to the world**. I just couldn't **get to sleep** last night for some reason.
Lukas:	Oh, no. Well, why don't we just call it a day and we can start again tomorrow? This will give you time to **recharge your batteries**.
Aria:	Thanks, but I think if I can just **grab a power nap**, then I'll feel much better.
Lukas:	No, go home and **get a good night's sleep**. Then we can just pick this up tomorrow.
Aria:	OK. I appreciate that. I'll **be good as new** tomorrow!

Janelle:	Are you OK?
Max:	Sure. Why?
Janelle:	You look a little tired.
Max:	Oh, I'**m wide awake** now, but I had a hard time **falling asleep** last night.
Janelle:	Are That's too bad. What was going on?
Max:	I don't know. I think I must have a lot of my mind. I **had a bad dream**, and then I couldn't **get back to sleep**.
Janelle:	That happens to me sometimes. How long were you able to sleep in the end?
Max:	Only about four hours or so.
Janelle:	Did you get up early?
Max:	Yes. Actually, I've been up since **the crack of dawn.**
Janelle:	Why is that?
Max:	I had a breakfast meeting, so I had to get up early. I **set my alarm** for 5:30 but I didn't get out of bed until almost 6:00. I **hit the snooze button** three times. I almost overslept!

Self-check 1

Circle the correct words.

Falling 1) **sleep / to sleep / asleep** sounds easy, yet for many people it can be a real challenge. Try these tips the next time you need to get 2) **to sleep / to sleepy / asleep**, or the next time you wake up and can't 3) get **up / back / down** to sleep.

- Have a nightly ritual. Go to sleep at the same time every night. And then wake up at the same time every morning.

- Do something that relaxes you before bedtime. Yoga, a hot shower or some soft music may all help you to get a good 4) **night / nights / night's** sleep.

- Avoid things that will keep you wide 5) **wake / woke / awake**. Don't exercise or drink coffee with caffeine right before bedtime.

- It may seem like a good idea to idea to 6) **sleep / grab / do** a power nap during the day, but be careful. It may make it harder for you to sleep at night.

- If you find yourself tossing and 7) **sleeping / walking / turning**, unable to sleep, get out of bed and sit in a chair until you are sleepy.

Self-check 2

Unscramble the words to make sentences. There is one extra word in each set that is not needed.

1 had / dream / bad / she / a / sleepy

   _____.

2 get / sleep / he / of / wink / didn't / a / eye

   _____.

3 map / new / after / good / was / as / my / I

   _____.

4 she / set / to / alarm / forgot / her / be

   _____.

5 the / go / button / I / always / hit / snooze

   _____.

6   to / feel / sleep / world / we / the / dead

_____.

7   batteries / I / recharge / need / to / my / get

_____.

8   the / up / morning / I / got / dawn / of / at / crack

_____.

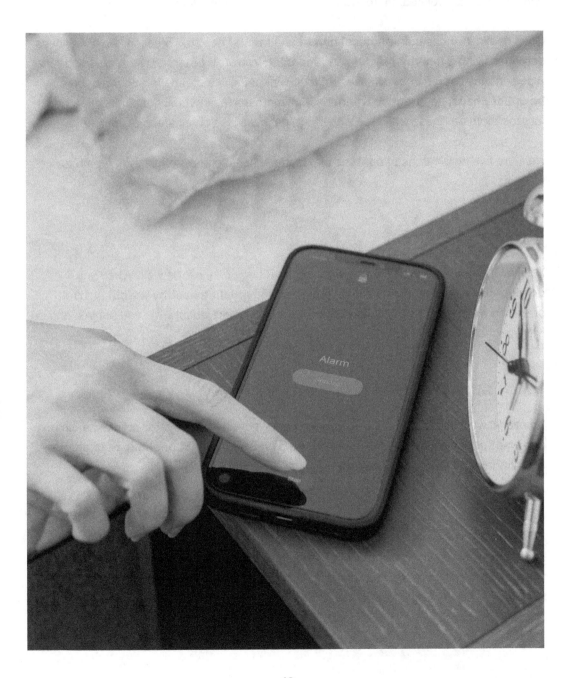

Unit 18
Health

Health and Wellness

Health and wellness. You may have seen these two words used as if they are the same. Although they are related, there are key differences between them.

Good health includes both **physical health** and **mental health**. The definition of wellness describes living a **healthy lifestyle** and **reaching your full potential**. Both are important. A person may be free from disease, but their well-being is suffering. Another person may **be out of shape,** yet **practise wellness** that improves their overall health. In short, health focuses more on illness while the idea of wellness focuses on all areas of your life.

Here are five major areas of our lives that matter when it comes to following a path to wellness.

Physical Wellness

You may be free from **aches and pains**, but your body may not be well. When you **do vigorous exercise**, spend time in nature and **maintain a healthy weight**, you're practicing wellness. This includes all the choices you make about what you put into and do with your body.

Emotional Wellness

Emotional wellness is a practice you engage in to increase your overall mental health and **emotional well-being**. You might do this by **nurturing relationships, establishing boundaries** and **learning to say no**.

Intellectual Wellness

Intellectual wellness is concerned with how you use your brain to **keep your mind sharp**. Practices that can increase your intellectual wellness include reading more, taking up a new hobby and learning a new language.

Occupational Wellness

Many of us spend a large part of our day at work, so it's important that we have occupational wellness. If you are not satisfied at work, you don't usually need to **quit your job** or change careers. You may just need to establish healthier relationships.

Social Wellness

Your social wellness is key to being a **healthy individual**. This means you take time for social events. It doesn't mean saying yes to everything. Learning when to go out with others and when to stay home is key to balancing your social wellness.

Self-check 1

Complete the sentences with words from the box. Two words are not used.

do	establish	keep	learn	live
maintain	practise	quit	reach	work

1   Alice will never _____ her full potential if she doesn't make some changes in her life.

2   I don't want to _____ my job. I love what I do. I just need to find a way to work smarter.

3   Your colleagues will take advantage of you if you don't _____ boundaries with them.

4   I'm neither heavy nor thin. I have always been able to _____ a healthy weight.

5   One way to _____ your mind sharp is to do a variety of word and number puzzles.

6   When will I _____ to say no? One again I've agreed to do something I don't want to do.

7   It's not always easy but it's important to _____ wellness in your life.

8   You'll lose weight faster if you _____ vigorous exercise. You need to get your heart rate up.

Self-check 2

Each sentence has an error. Replace the ~~crossed out~~ word.

1 If you have a ~~health~~ _____ lifestyle now, you will be more likely to be healthier later.

2 Greg has worked hard to raise the awareness of ~~mind~~ _____ health issues.

3 Henri is out ~~to~~ _____ shape, so he joined a gym and hired a personal trainer.

4 Any ~~healthful~~ _____ individual should be able to perform these job duties.

5 Friendships can be fragile, so it's important to ~~reach~~ _____ relationships.

6 I've been very concerned about Lila's emotional ~~good-being~~ _____ since her breakup.

7 This isn't Glen's usual aches and ~~sores~~ _____, but something far more serious.

8 My grandmother is in excellent ~~body~~ _____ health for her age.

Unit 19
Emotions

Hideo: Did you hear about Ricardo?

Kathy: No. Is he OK?

Hideo: Yeah, but he recently lost his job at the restaurant. He started working there over 20 years ago.

Kathy: Oh, no! How **terribly sad**. And he had no idea this was going to happen?

Hideo: He said he **had a nagging feeling** that something was wrong, but he didn't think he was in danger of losing his job. I know he was **deeply hurt** with how they told him. They sent him an email.

Kathy: No way! Really?

Hideo: I'm **totally serious**. An email! Isn't that so unprofessional? This is how they treat a long-time employee.

Kathy: Well, I'm sure he can get a job with all his experience.

Hideo: I hope you're right, but I think that's **wildly optimistic**. A lot of restaurants have closed down recently. He's **scared to death** he won't be able to get a job in this economy.

Kathy: I think he will be **pleasantly surprised**. A lot of people in the restaurant industry know Ricardo is a good worker. He has an excellent reputation.

Chloe: Congratulations! I heard you won the top prize for your essay.

Sven: I did! I'm **absolutely thrilled**.

Chloe: Did you have any idea that you might win?

Sven: None at all. It really **took me by surprise**. I'm **utterly amazed** that I was even considered a finalist.

Chloe: Who told you about the contest anyway?

Sven: My academic advisor suggested I enter. I'm **eternally grateful** to her for her support and advice. The process was not easy. I was **hopelessly confused** at first by what to do, but she really helped me figure everything out.

Chloe: Did you accept the prize in person?

Sven: Yeah, they had an awards ceremony over the weekend. I **was filled with fear,** to be honest, because I had to give a speech. I'd never given a speech before.

Chloe: Well, if you can write an award-winning essay then you can write and deliver a speech.

Sven: That's what my advisor said! She said it was **perfectly normal** to feel anxious. I do think it helped to **raise my self-esteem**, so I'm pleased about that.

Self-check 1

Match the parts. Then use the phrases to complete the sentences.

deeply	confused
absolutely	hurt
eternally	thrilled
hopelessly	grateful
wildly	sad
terribly	normal
perfectly	surprised
pleasantly	optimistic

1 She was _____ by what he said. She left in tears.

2 Alex was _____ that Jill finally agreed to marry him.

3 I'm _____ by this math problem. Can how to solve it?

4 Thank you for believing in me. I'll be _____ to you.

5 Kip's death was _____. I had no idea he was even ill.

6 I did not expect to win, so when I did I was _____.

7 It's _____ to feel nervous. Everyone feels some anxiety.

8 The stock sold for $12, not $60. Her prediction was _____.

Self-check 2

Unscramble the words to make sentences. There is one extra word in each set that is not needed.

1 is / by / amazed / Peter / grade / utterly / his / hopelessly

   _____.

2 pleasantly / about / is / Valerie / totally / quitting / serious

   _____.

3 experience / join / my / raised / the / self-esteem

   _____.

4 nagging / about / have / this / I / a / feeling / perfect

   _____.

5 filled / was / Wendy / with / fear / optimistic

   _____.

6 surprise / email / me / by / thrill / your / took

   _____.

7 death / was / Jacqueline / to / afraid / scared

   _____.

Unit 20
Fashion

Dressing for Success

People make a judgment of you within five to seven seconds of meeting you. Recent research suggests it may be closer to three seconds. It doesn't matter if you are meeting your in-laws, interviewing for a job, or running a business meeting, you don't have long to make a good first impression.

Coco Chanel once said, 'Dress shabbily and they remember the dress; dress impeccably and they remember the woman'. If you want people to see you as successful, then you need to **dress the part**. People who **take pride in their appearance** tend to be feel more confident. People admire well-dressed individuals and see them as leaders. **Proper attire** also helps you to create an image. Others will see you as someone who cares about how they look.

But how do we dress for success? It may be easier than you think, and it certainly doesn't need to cost a lot. You undoubtedly don't need a **whole new wardrobe**, but you probably do need some upgrades. A good starting point is going to your closet and seeing what clothes you already have. If you haven't worn an **item of clothing** for a long time or it**'s out of fashion**, get rid of it.

See what classics are missing. These are going to be a better investment than **the latest fashion** that you probably won't wear very often. These include simple shirts and blouses, and dark suits, dresses and skirts.

When you're ready to go shopping, choose quality over quantity. Try to purchase the best clothing that you can afford. It's better to have one quality item that will last a long time than three lesser-quality items. You don't have to buy **designer labels**. It's fine to **buy off the rack**, but look for higher-end items on sale.

Choose items with **neutral colours** that you can **mix and match** easily. Try to dress for where you want to go, not just where you are. If you don't **have an eye for** fashion or are unsure what to buy, bring a friend along or ask for help.

It's also important to consider what clothing is appropriate for different situations. Jeans, a T-shirt and sandals are **casual attire** and may be fine for some informal occasions, but probably not at work. According to a recent survey, hoodies, strapless dresses, flip flops, short skirts, and ripped jeans were all viewed as inappropriate for most workplaces.

Finally, just because you dress for success does not mean you can't be **fashion forward** or be yourself. Think about your **sense of style** and what you enjoy wearing. Accessorizing your look with the right scarf, tie, jacket or briefcase is an easy way to make any look your own.

Self-check 1

Circle the correct word. Then use the phrases to complete the sentences.

join / mix / grab and match
look / buy / pay off the rack
be / do / make out of fashion
dress / wear / take the part
have / look / dress an eye for fashion
be / make / take pride in one's appearance

1 If you want to become a manager someday, then _____ of a manager.

2 It's important to _____ and look good, including maintaining good hygiene.

3 I wouldn't buy that cap. It's cute now but I think it will _____ soon.

4 Buy clothes that you can _____ so you can create lots of new outfits.

5 Kit and Anita _____. People ask them for fashion advice all the time.

6 Mia's wealthy and has all of her clothes made for her. She won't ever
_____.

Self-check 2

Complete the Q&A with words from the box. One word is not used.

attire	designer	forward	item	latest	neutral
	proper	rack	sense	whole	

This week fashion editor Louella Tan answers questions from our online readers.

Q: Is casual 1)_____ OK for a job interview?

A: No! You should dress professionally for any interview. 2)_____ attire for most interviews would be a suit. It needn't be the 3)_____ fashion. Just wear nice but conservative clothing.

Q: I just got a new job and now need a 4)_____ new wardrobe. Where do I start?

A: See what in your closet you can still wear. Buy clothes with 5)_____ colours, and mix and match items to save money. You don't need 6)_____ labels – just buy quality items on sale.

Q: I want to be more fashion 7)_____. But how?

A: Just being true to your own 8)_____ of style. No 9)_____ of clothing will make a huge difference. It's the overall look and attitude that will catch the envious eyes of other people.

Unit 21
Time

Kurt:	Hey, Lisa. Sorry to bother you, but do you **have a minute**?
Lisa:	Sure, Kurt. Let me just finish this email up ...
Kurt:	No problem. **Take your time**.
Lisa:	... OK. Done. What can I help you with?
Kurt:	I'm **having a hard time** finishing up this proposal, and I was wondering if you **had extra time** over the next few days to help me complete it. I hate to ask, but I'm really **pressed for time**.
Lisa:	Well, as you know I have a pretty **demanding schedule** these days, but I think I can probably **make time** for this.
Kurt:	Oh, what a relief! That's great to hear. I've just been so **incredibly busy** lately. I don't really want to go to our boss and explain that I couldn't get it done.
Lisa:	Don't worry. I'm sure if we put our heads together we can finish it up.

Eva:	I have my exam tomorrow. I really hope I do well on it.
Raul:	Oh, I'm sure you will.
Eva:	You've taken this exam before. Do you have any advice for me?
Raul:	Let's see ... Well, of course make absolutely sure you'**re on time**. I don't know if they'll even let you take the exam if you're late.
Eva:	Got it.
Raul:	And you should already be familiar with the types of questions on this exam. You don't want to **waste time** reading through all the instruction lines.
Eva:	I've taken a lot of practice exams, so that shouldn't be a problem for me.
Raul:	Oh, this is a good tip. Before you begin, **spend time** quickly looking over the whole exam. This will be **time well spent**. Then there will be no surprises and you can pace yourself.
Eva:	Right, good to know.
Raul:	And be sure to **keep your eye on the clock**. You don't want to **run out of time** at the end and not finish. But if you happen to **have spare time** at the end, go back over your answers and check them carefully.

Self-check 1

Circle the correct words.

1   Don't be late. Be sure to **keep / watch / take** your eye on the clock.

2   Review your notes before your exam. It will be time well **pressed / saved / spent**.

3   I'm exhausted. I've been so **demanding / incredibly / hard** busy these past few weeks.

4   What do you do in your **pressed / spare / schedule** time? Do you have any hobbies?

5   Do you have a **time / clock / minute**? I could really use a hand with this presentation.

6   I try to **spend / save / do** time with my grandparents every other weekend.

7   Jill has a very **spare / demanding / pressed** schedule this week. It will be hard to make an appointment with her.

Self-check 2

Complete the sentences with words from the box. Two words are not used.

extra	had	kept	made	ran	on	pressed
	took	wasted	went			

1   Wendy _____ a hard time figuring out that problem.

2   I never finished the exam. I'm afraid I _____ out of time.

3   Kat _____ time on silly things in her youth. Sadly, she never even finished high school.

4   It was hard to make a decision. I _____ my time and considered all the options.

5   The concert didn't start _____ time. The band was an hour late!

6   If you have _____ time this weekend, feel free to give me a call.

7   If you are _____ for time, I'll be happy to write up the meeting notes.

8   I had to study all day, but I _____ time for some exercise that evening.

Unit 22
News

A Fuzzy Truth

Even if you've never read a **tabloid newspaper**, the headlines probably **grab your attention** at the supermarket checkout. From celebrity stories to the truly wacky, tabloids cover stories that are outside the field of serious journalism.

Newspapers like *The New York Times* and *The Guardian* are known for their **fair reporting**. Their journalists **report on the news** and are known for being objective. They **check their facts** and **confirm their sources**. In other words, they follow journalistic standards. Tabloids tend not to follow any of these rules. So where do they get their stories from?

Often tabloids simply **make up their stories**. If a story is about an incredible event or the people in the story are not easily identified, then it may be **fake news**. Something doesn't have to be true for a publisher to **run a story**. Someone just has to say that it's true.

Good tabloid writers expand upon small news items in the back pages of traditional newspapers. In fact, one big difference between tabloid newsrooms and those at serious newspapers is that tabloid writers don't do much work outside the office. Once a writer finds a story, they may simply call family members or people involved with the story to get quotes. Using those quotes, the writer **fleshes out the story** and makes it more about the people involved than the events themselves.

Celebrity news is a staple of the tabloids, and sources for this information include security guards, hair stylists and even police officers. These people call the writer when they have an **inside story** on a celebrity. But a lot of tabloid celebrity news actually comes from celebrities themselves. They may not always want to **go on record** and may even choose to **leak a story** to a tabloid because its readers may be less likely to believe the story. It's also free publicity.

So the next time you see a tabloid, **check the headlines**. How much do *you* believe?

English Collocations in Context

Self-check 1

Complete the sentences with words from the box. Two words are not used.

> check   fair   fake   flesh   grab   inside
> kill   leak   run   tabloid

1 A story that is gained from first-hand experience is called a(n) _____ story.

2 The purpose of a good headline is to _____ the reader's attention.

3 A(n) _____ newspaper is one that doesn't follow solid journalistic standards.

4 To see what a news story is about, simply _____ the headline.

5 News that is clearly false or misleading is known as _____ news.

6 Serious newspapers are well-known for their _____ reporting.

7 If a publisher decides to _____ a story, it means they plan to publish it.

8 Writers _____ out a story when they need to further develop it.

Self-check 2

Circle the correct words.

1 **A:** Can I use your name in my news story?
   B: No, I'd rather not publicly **have a / go on / go to** record.

2 **A:** Read this. Do you think it could possibly be true?
   B: No way. The reporter obviously **ran / made up / leaked** the story.

3 **A:** Are we prepared to publish this story?
   B: Not quite. We should ask the reporter to **confirm / report on / run** her sources first.

4 **A:** How does everyone already know about these political appointments?
   B: Someone must have **checked / fleshed out / leaked** the story to the press.

5 **A:** My dream is to **report on / grab / run** the news for an international media company.
   B: Well, good luck. I know how hard it is to work in journalism these days.

6 **A:** Who wrote this? This data can't be right.
   B: Let me ask the reporter to **check / learn / agree** his facts again.

Unit 23
Dining out

Olivia:	How was your meal?
Stavros:	It was great. Thanks for bringing me to this place.
Olivia:	I'm glad you liked it. Say, do you want to **split a dessert**?
Stavros:	A dessert?
Olivia:	Yeah. We could **look over the menu** again and see what looks good.
Stavros:	I couldn't eat another bite. I actually need to get going soon.
Olivia:	No problem. Let's **ask for the bill**.
Stavros:	Good idea.
Olivia:	See if you can **catch the attention of** our server.
Stavros:	OK. Do you want **separate checks**?
Olivia:	No, we can just get one. You know what? I'll **pick up the tab** if you **leave a tip**.
Stavros:	Really? You don't have to do that.
Olivia:	I'm happy to.
Stavros:	Well, thank you. I'll get dinner next time we go out.

Kirk:	Are there any nice restaurants in your neighbourhood?
Junko:	There are a few.
Kirk:	How often do you go out to eat?
Junko:	Oh, probably once or twice a week.
Kirk:	What kind of place do you go to?
Junko:	I don't eat meat, so I have to make sure any restaurant has **vegetarian options**. I often go to a nice café that**'s within walking distance** of where I live. It's called Green Garden.
Kirk:	Is it a **fine-dining restaurant**?
Junko:	No, not at all. It's a **casual restaurant**. A lot of students go there. It **has a cool vibe**.
Kirk:	What do you usually order?
Junko:	It has an **extensive menu**, but I usually get their **daily special**. It's always good.
Kirk:	Any favourites?
Junko:	Their veggie pad thai is fantastic. It has tofu, rice noodles, green onions, bean sprouts, roasted peanuts –
Junko:	Stop! You're **making my mouth water**.
Kirk:	I didn't know you liked Thai food. I'll be happy to take you there sometime.
Junko:	You know, I could eat now …

English Collocations in Context

Self-check 1

Circle the correct word. Then use the phrases to complete the sentences.

pick up / split / leave a dessert
ask / leave / have a tip
catch / split / look over the menu
pick up / buy / order the tab
make / ask for / eat the bill
have / see / add a cool vibe

1 The two new cafés near our house both _____.

2 In some countries it's customary to _____ of about 15%.

3 I need a few minutes to _____ before I place my order.

4 If you are finished with your dessert I'll go ahead and _____.

5 I'm full, but I do want something sweet. Why don't we
_____?

6 You paid for my meal last time, so let me _____ today.

Self-check 2

Each sentence has an error. Replace the ~~crossed out~~ word.

1 Vito's is not a ~~good~~ _____-dining restaurant, but the food is still good.

2 Lebanese Kitchen has an extensive ~~bill~~ _____ of healthy dishes.

3 The ~~day~~ _____ special here is delicious, and very good value.

4 I'd like to eat somewhere that has a lot of vegetarian ~~menus~~ _____.

5 Let's ask the server to give us ~~divided~~ _____ checks.

6 Maria's Cantina is within walking ~~distant~~ _____ of campus

7 All the fresh bread at this café is making my mouth ~~wet~~ _____.

8 I don't want to get dressed up, so let's just eat at any ~~cause~~ _____ restaurant.

9 Try to ~~ask~~ _____ the attention of the server if she comes by again.

Unit 24
Environment

Environmental Challenges

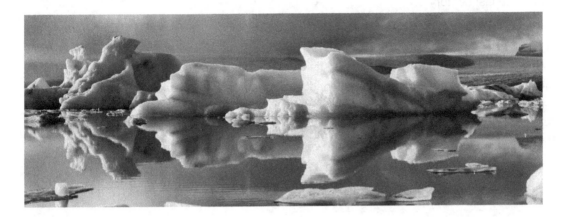

Overpopulation. **Urban sprawl**. Overfishing. **Rising temperatures**. We here at *Tune In* magazine know that these are just a few of the many challenges plaguing our planet. In your opinion, what is the biggest environmental problem facing the world today?

The biggest problem has to be **climate change**, and more specifically **global warming**, which leads to higher temperatures in the oceans and at the Earth' surface. The **climate crisis** is causing tropical storms and other weather events such as hurricanes, heat waves and flooding to be more intense and frequent. A recent heatwave in Antarctica saw a marked temperature increase. The Greenland ice sheet is melting **at an alarming rate**. Scientists warn that the planet may soon **reach a tipping point**, which will have **catastrophic consequences**.

– Paula, 31, Curitiba, Brazil

To me it's **food waste**. We waste about a third of the food that is intended for human consumption. That's enough to feed 3 billion people! It's different depending on where you live. In developing countries, 40% of food waste occurs after it is harvested. In developed countries, 40% occurs at the retail and consumer levels. In the developed world especially, a lot of food is wasted simply because of how it looks. In the US, more than 50% of all produce is thrown away because it's seen as 'ugly'. Some countries are beginning to address this problem at last by creating guidelines and **passing laws**.

– Dimitri, 42, Kazan, Russia

I worry about **habitat loss** and the impact this has on both healthy populations of animals as well as on **endangered species**. The population sizes of mammals, birds, reptiles and birds have declined an average of 68% over the past 50 years. This biodiversity loss is mostly due to habitat loss to make way for agriculture. There is even talk of another mass extinction of wildlife. More than 500 species of land animals are **on the brink of extinction**. They are likely to be lost within 20 years – the same number that were lost over the last century.

– Laurel, 31, Birmingham, UK

Unsustainable **farming practices** and rising temperatures have led to an increasing threat of **water insecurity**. Just 3% of the world's water is fresh water, and most of that is frozen in glaciers or otherwise unavailable for use. In terms of farming, billions of tons of top soil are lost every year. This soil is often full of fertilisers, which can contaminate fresh water. The soil is also vulnerable to wind and water erosion. In short, more than a billion people lack regular access to fresh water, and it's not getting better.

– Khalid, 18, Oran, Algeria

Self-check 1

Match the parts. Then use the phrases to complete the sentences.

endangered	loss
farming	practices
food	species
habitat	sprawl
rising	temperatures
urban	waste

1   The _____ at the poles has caused the ice caps to melt at a faster rate.

2   _____ is the disappearance of natural environments for plants and animals.

3   Besides being ugly, the _____ has led to the overreliance on the automobile.

4   The gray wolf is no longer considered a(n) _____ in the United States.

5   Two common _____ are crop rotation and the use of natural fertilisers.

6   I work in the restaurant industry and see _____ all the time. We throw out boxes of fruits and vegetables every day.

Self-check 2

Circle the correct words.

1   Water **waste / insecurity / practices** refers to the lack of a reliable source of water.

2   Climate scientists say we must limit **climate / weather / global** warming to 1.5 degrees Celsius by 2040 to avoid disaster.

3   We have a serious climate **brink / point / crisis** on our hands, and the world has to work together to tackle it head on.

4   It's fine to **pass / call / reach** laws, but it will take more than that to change people's behaviours.

5   The Earth's temperature has risen **at / with / through** an alarming rate over the past century.

6   The rise in sea levels will have catastrophic **issues / consequences / causes** on coastal communities all over the world.

7   Some people claim that **climate / weather / global** change is not real, but these people should not be taken seriously.

8   Many nations may soon **make / touch / reach** a tipping point in their attitude toward the environment.

9   The Giant Ibis is a bird species **on / to / in** the brink of extinction.

Unit 25
Relationships

Matt:	You husband Karl seems really nice.
Natalia:	Oh, he's great.
Matt:	How did you two meet?
Natalia:	We **met through a friend**. My friend Rusty knew Karl from school, so he introduced us.
Matt:	That's nice. Was the **love at first sight**?
Natalia:	Well, not exactly, but I think we did **have chemistry**, and still do! We **went on a date** and got along really well.
Matt:	Was it a **blind date**?
Natalia:	Actually it was, and I was really nervous about it. It turned out fine, though. We **have a lot in common**.
Matt:	I think that's really important if you want a **healthy relationship**.
Natalia:	I agree.
Matt:	So you'd say you **see eye to eye** on the important things in life?
Natalia:	I think so.
Matt:	That's good. How long did you date before you got married?
Natalia:	About two years. We're about to **celebrate our anniversary** in fact.
Matt:	Nice! How many years have you been married?
Natalia:	This will be our five-year anniversary.
Matt:	Are you doing anything special?
Natalia:	We are. We're going to Italy. We **went** to Venice **on our honeymoon** and have been wanting to go back ever since. So what about you, Matt? Are you **seeing anyone**?
Matt:	I've been in a relationship with a woman called Chloe for about eight months now. Things are going pretty well.
Natalia:	Awesome!
Matt:	It is, but we're not ready to **make a commitment** or anything just yet. We want to see how things go.
Natalia:	That makes sense. There's no point in rushing things. How did you meet?
Matt:	We just **met by chance**. We were in the same spin class at the gym. We just started chatting one day. She was in a **long-distance relationship** at the time, but I guess things weren't going that well.

Natalia:	So one thing led to another!
Matt:	Well, I suppose. We went out for coffee a few times, and things eventually started to get serious.
Natalia:	I hope to meet her sometime.
Matt:	Well, maybe the four of us can do something together. It could be kind of a **double date**!
Natalia:	Ha! I'd love that!

Self-check I

Circle the correct word. Then use the phrases to complete the sentences.

be / celebrate / have chemistry
see / meet / make by chance
go / see / double on a date
see / make / love a commitment
so / have / see eye to eye
see / work / have a lot in common

1 Marta and I _____. We both love sports, movies and travel.

2 Luciana is going to _____ with Ken. It will be her first since her divorce.

3 Paxton and I didn't _____. A friend of his introduced us.

4 Fran and Adam _____ as a couple. I can't describe it, but it's there.

5 If you want to keep Zoe, you have to _____ soon. She won't wait forever.

6 Mei-ling and I don't _____ on how to raise kids. That could be a problem.

English Collocations in Context

Self-check 2

Circle the correct words.

Welcome to Happy Couples, Inc. Please answer these questions to help us find your perfect match.

1   Do you believe in love **in / at / with** first sight?

2   What do you think makes a **health / healthy / health-wise** relationship?

3   Do you think a **far / much / long**-distance relationship can ever work?

4   Have you ever been on a **twice / double / two** date?

5   What's a good way for someone to **engage / play / celebrate** their anniversary?

6   Do you know any couples who met **through / by / at** a friend?

7   Where would you like to go **to / on / with** your honeymoon?

8   Are you **seeing / lying / crushing** anyone at the moment?

9   Would you ever consider going on a blind **match / couple / date**?

Unit 26
Communication

Types of Communication

Communication is the act of sharing information. There are many ways to do this. You might use verbal communication when you **make small talk** with someone, written communication when you text someone, nonverbal communication when you show how you feel about something, and visual communication when you share a GIF or video online. Here's a more **in-depth look** at these four areas of communication, and some suggestions for developing your **communication skills.**

Nonverbal

Nonverbal communication is the use of **facial expressions**, gestures and **body language** to **convey information**. This type of communication is helpful when trying to understand others' thoughts and feelings. For example, if someone crosses their arms they may be feeling anxious or defensive. If they **make eye contact** they are probably feeling confident and open to communicating. To improve your own nonverbal communication skills, try to notice how your emotions affect you. Be intentional in how you communicate nonverbally, and make an effort to display positive body language when you feel good about something.

Verbal

Verbal communication uses language through speaking or **sign language**. It's often used during video conferences, phone calls and of course **face-to-face conversations**. When you **engage in a conversation**, speak with confidence. **Project your voice** so your ideas are clear and easy to understand. Avoid words like 'yeah' and 'like'. Words like these can be distracting for the listener. In addition, be aware of how well you listen to others. Doing so will help you become a more **effective communicator**.

Written

Written communication involves using symbols like letters and numbers to convey information. It is especially useful because it provides a record of information. To develop your written communication skills, strive for clarity and simplicity. Focus on the main message and think about the reader. Include details only if they are needed.

And be careful about your tone. When something is only written, it can be misunderstood easily. For example, when you **tell a joke** or use sarcasm, the meaning or intention may be lost.

Visual

Visual communication is the act of using photos, drawings, emojis, graphs and other images to **communicate a message**. Visuals are often used when you **give a presentation** because it provides context alongside other forms of communication. To develop your visual communication skills, always consider your audience. Include visuals that are easily understood. For example, if you are showing a graph with data, take the time to explain what is happening in the visual and how it relates to what you are saying.

Self-check I

Complete the conversation with words from the box. Two words are not used.

> communicate   convey   engage   give   make
>
> make   project   speak   talk   tell

Lucinda: I have to 1)_____ a presentation to our sales team next week. I'm kind of nervous about it.

Mario: You're a good speaker. Why would you be nervous?

Lucinda: I can chat one-on-one and 2)_____ small talk with others easily. But I get anxious when I have to stand in front of a group and speak.

Mario: Well, I can offer you some advice if you like. The main thing is to remember you are there to 3)_____ a message. Be sure your presentation is clear and easy to follow.

Lucinda: I think my presentation is fine. My boss even OK'd it.

Mario: That's good! Then I would just focus on your delivery. 4)_____ your voice so everyone can hear you easily, and be sure to 5)_____ eye contact. It's the best way to connect with your audience.

Lucinda: Should I 6)_____ a joke at the beginning?

Mario: That's a great way to put people at ease. Just remember you are there to 7)_____ information, so make sure your message comes through loud and clear.

Lucinda: What about taking questions? Should I take them during the presentation?

Mario: That's up to you. Personally, I prefer to wait until the end. If you 8)_____ in a conversation with your audience before you finish your talk, it may throw off your timing.

Self-check 2

Circle the correct words.

1 Employers want employees with excellent **talk / communication / speak** skills.

2 You can usually tell what Jon is thinking by his **face-to-face / facing / facial** expressions.

3 An important part of communication is body **conversation / talk / language**.

4 We need to take an in-depth **look / sight / call** at our company's email policies.

5 There are groups that can help you to be a more effective **talker / communicator / speech**.

6 When I don't speak the local language, I use **sign / hand / gesture** language to communicate.

7 I'm not crazy about texting. I prefer to have a **facial / two-faced / face-to-face** conversation.

Unit 27
Size

Luke:	Look at this article. It says a **considerable number** of **corporate giants** don't pay any taxes, or very little.
Mae-lin:	That's terrible.
Luke:	It is. I know many of those companies make **huge profits** every year.
Mae-lin:	It's not fair. Some of those companies say that they help by reinvesting profits and creating jobs. But I don't think that's a **strong argument**.
Luke:	Well, companies like that wield **great power**, so what can you do?
Mae-lin:	I'm not sure.
Luke:	I would think a **large proportion** of the population expects all companies to pay their fair share.
Mae-lin:	I blame the government for not enforcing their tax laws.
Luke:	Maybe we should stop paying our taxes, and see what happens.
Mae-lin:	That would be a **big mistake**.
Luke:	I'm not really serious. But it is frustrating.

Inga:	I'm going to order takeaway. Do you want anything?
Shane:	Um, sure. Can you order me a small salad?
Inga:	That's it?
Shane:	Yeah. I'm trying to **lose weight**. I've started to **limit the size** of my food portions.
Inga:	Why?
Shane:	My diet lately has been awful. I've started reading food labels, and see there are a **huge number** of calories in many foods.
Inga:	I think you look fine, but good for you.
Shane:	I know I've been eating a lot of food that is **high in fat** lately, and I just want to **watch my weight** more.
Inga:	Well, I have **great admiration** for you. I know it's never easy to diet.
Shane:	I'm doing OK. I'm also exercising, so that helps a lot. I've already lost about five kilos. It's not much, but …
Inga:	That's a **big accomplishment**. You should feel good about that.
Shane:	Oh, I do, but I have a way to go until I get to my **ideal weight**.

Self-check 1

Unscramble the words to make sentences. There is one extra word in each set that is not needed.

1   to / lose / I / size / weight / need

_____.

2   that / has / power / big / company / great

_____.

3   strong / group / the / size / limit / of / the

_____.

4   is / huge / a / million / number / a / size

_____.

5   weight / my / watch / to / I / want / see

_____.

6   a / light / number / that's / considerable

_____.

7   always / profits / make / huge / they / heavy

_____.

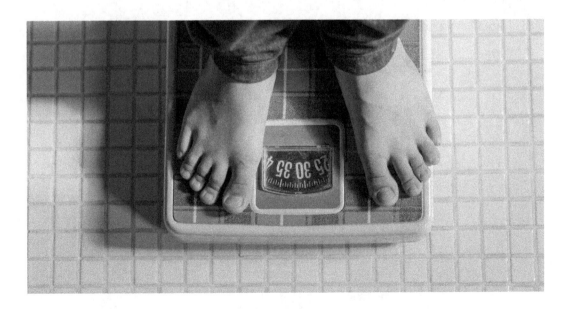

Self-check 2

Match the parts. Then use the phrases to complete the definitions.

ideal	in fat
high	weight
big	argument
strong	accomplishment
big	giant
corporate	proportion
great	admiration
large	mistake

1   Please don't copy someone else's essay. That would be a(n) _____.

2   Jess completed a marathon last weekend. What a(n) _____!

3   I have _____ for people who can study and work at the same time.

4   What is the _____ of a 30-year-old male who is 180 cm tall?

5   It's not a(n) _____ to just say you did it because you knew you wouldn't get caught.

6   A(n) _____ of the survey respondents said they approve of the new government.

7   I wouldn't order the sesame chicken. It's very _____ because of all the oil.

8   A(n) _____ like that has a responsibility to pay fair wages to its employees.

Unit 28
Celebrations

Eid al-Fitr

Eid al-Fitr is an important religious holiday celebrated by Muslims worldwide. It's a **national holiday** in many countries with large Muslim populations. During the holy month of Ramadan, Muslims fast from sun up to sundown to honor the month that the Quran was revealed to the Prophet Mohammed. Eid al-Fitr is a **cause for celebration** that **marks the end of** Ramadan.

During Eid al-Fitr Muslims get together with their friends and family to **give thanks** to Allah following the previous month of reflection. The holiday **serves as a reminder** to be grateful for what one has and to share with those who are less fortunate.

The exact start date is usually not certain in advance. It depends on when the crescent moon is first sighted. This can create an **atmosphere of excitement** as people wait. The holiday can be delayed by a day if clouds cover the moon or if the sky is too bright when the moon is out. This is why Ramadan can start on different days in different parts of the world. Some Muslims **celebrate the holiday** when the new moon appears over Mecca instead of their own locations.

Celebrations typically last for one to three days, depending on the country. People wear traditional clothes, either purchasing them or making them themselves. They take part in special morning prayers in mosques or outdoor areas. They **offer greetings** of 'Eid Mubarak', or 'Have a blessed Eid,' throughout the day. They get together with loved ones to prepare and eat special foods. They **express gratitude** for what they have. Muslims also **make a donation** to the poor. Some people **do volunteer work** at community centres or hand out their own food to those in need. Muslims are also encouraged to give and **seek forgiveness** during Eid al-Fitr.

English Collocations in Context

Giving gifts is a big part of Eid celebrations. Children receive money and sweets such as biscuits and dates are exchanged among family, friends, neighbours, colleagues and even strangers. Family members also **exchange gifts**, though most gifts are saved for the youngest members in each family.

As well as the universal traditions, there are other ones in different countries. Some countries **hold events** to celebrate the holiday. For example, people in United Arab Emirates gather to watch fireworks. In Turkey, people visit cemeteries to **pay their respects** to the dead. In Afghanistan, a popular Eid activity is to paint hard-boiled eggs and have a food fight with them.

Self-check 1

Complete the text with words from the box. Two words are not used.

> celebrate   do   exchange   express   hold
>
> make   national   seek   serve   thanks

Thanksgiving Day is a **1)**_____ holiday in the United States. It's the fourth Thursday in November. Many Americans take a day of vacation on the following Friday to make a four-day weekend. People may travel long distances to **2)**_____ the holiday with family and friends.

The holiday dates back to 1621, the year after a group known as the Pilgrims arrived in Massachusetts from England. After a difficult winter, they turned for help to neighbouring Native Americans, who taught them how to plant corn and other crops. The next autumn's harvest inspired the Pilgrims to **3)**_____ their gratitude by holding a feast.

Thanksgiving dinner almost always includes some of the foods served at that first feast, such as turkey, potatoes, pumpkin pie and cranberry sauce. Before the meal begins, people usually pause to give **4)**_____ for their blessings. People do not typically **5)**_____ gifts on this holiday. Rather, they all contribute something to the feast.

Some people **6)**_____ volunteer work, such as working at a community centre to help feed people who are homeless. Others may **7)**_____ a donation to charity during this time. Thanksgiving weekend is also the biggest shopping weekend of the year. Stores often **8)**_____ events to attract shoppers.

Self-check 2

Circle the correct words.

1   It's common in Spain to **speak / talk / offer** greetings of *Hola* any time of the day.

2   This is a day when people **do / seek / make** forgiveness for their past actions.

3   They went to the cemetery to **say / thank / pay** their respects to their ancestors.

4   Juneteenth is a day that **does / marks / expresses** the end of slavery in the US.

5   The fact that she made it home for the holiday is a **cause / special / join** for celebration.

6   It's New Year's Eve and there's a(n) **cloud / air / atmosphere** of excitement in the air.

7   Indigenous People's Day **serves / marks / holds** as a reminder of the people who were here long before Europeans arrived.

Unit 29
Technology

Nora:	What are you reading?
Sam:	It's an article on some of the **emerging technologies** we're seeing today.
Nora:	That sounds interesting.
Sam:	It is.
Nora:	What **technological developments** have made the biggest impact on your life?
Sam:	Wow, that's a great question. In my lifetime it would have to be the internet, of course. Younger people seem to have always had **high-speed internet**, but I remember when I sent my first email.
Nora:	Same here. And when I sent my first fax.
Sam:	There have been so many **advances in technology** since then that it's hard to keep up sometimes.
Nora:	How many **electronic devices** do you have?
Sam:	I just have my phone – that's it. I use it for everything. But I wouldn't say I'm necessarily **tech-savvy**. Say, maybe you can help with something. I want to **back up my files** to the cloud. I know it's **not rocket science**, but I don't know how to do it.
Nora:	Oh, I can show you how. It's easy.
Sam:	It's always easy when you know how!

Ahmed:	Is that your cat?
Haley:	Yes, it's my kitty cam.
Ahmed:	A what?
Haley:	I call it my kitty cam. I have several webcams at home so I can check on my cat while I'm here at work. I love to watch her play when I'm not around.
Ahmed:	That's cool. You're **light years ahead** of me when it comes to technologies like that.
Haley:	I can feed her too. Look, I **control it remotely.** I just click this and it dispenses some cat treats.
Ahmed:	How convenient. I should try to **adopt technology** like that.
Haley:	Well, this used to be **cutting-edge technology** I suppose, but these kinds of apps are very common nowadays. And they're very **user-friendly**.

Ahmed: Can I see the app?

Haley: Sure. These apps give me a real **sense of freedom**. I can start dinner before I get home. I can adjust the thermostat so my flat is cool when I get home. There are always new things you can do.

Ahmed: Do you **receive an alert** if someone rings your doorbell?

Haley: I do. And then I can see who is at the front door. I can then talk to the person if need be.

Self-check I

Circle the correct word. Then use the phrases to complete the sentences.

> back up my **technology / files / internet**
> light years **ahead / above / beyond**
> control **remotely / afar / distantly**
> cutting-edge **technology / internet / freedom**
> adopt **remotes / technology / devices**
> not rocket **technology / science / development**

1 The _____ in this computer allows it to process massive amounts of data.

2 I need to _____ in case I accidently delete or lose them.

3 Some businesses go out of business because they are too slow to _____.

4 The mobile technology used today is _____ of what I had as a kid.

5 I want a heating and cooling system that I can _____ when I'm at work.

6 It's easy to install a new operating system. It's _____.

Self-check 2

Circle the correct words.

1   I want to buy a smart watch that is stylish, inexpensive and **easy- / new- / user**-friendly.

2   I often have to ask IT for help at work as I'm not the most tech-**savvy / -fancy / -skillful** person.

3   High-**fast / -speed / -width** internet is the norm for many people these days.

4   I have three **electronic / techy / gadget** devices: my laptop, my phone and my tablet.

5   What are some emerging **data / technologies / users** that can help to reshape the economy?

6   There are recent **technological / progress / state** developments in the field of medicine.

7   If you want to have a **feel / sense / knowledge** of freedom, unplug for a week and get offline.

8   I **know / open / receive** an alert if someone tries to log in to my email account.

9   The advances **in / at / by** technology during the past few years have been remarkable.

Unit 30
Energy

Renewable Energy

Renewable energy comes from **natural sources** or sources that are constantly replenished. In other words, unlike **fossil fuels** like coal and gas, they are sources that we will never run out of. Humans have long harnessed **sustainable energy** for heating, lighting and transport. Now that we have cheaper and more innovative ways to capture nature's power, renewables are becoming an even more important **energy source** in our quest to **reduce our carbon footprint**. What are the main types of renewable energy in use today?

Solar

Sunlight is one of our planet's most abundant energy resources. The amount of solar energy that is available to us during one hour is more than the total amount of energy consumed worldwide in a year. It may sound like a perfect renewable energy source, but one challenge is that the amount of solar energy varies according to season, time of day and location. Another challenge is the cost of building cost-effective **solar panels**. Yet another challenge is storage.

Wind

Wind is another plentiful source of energy. Wind energy turns a turbine's blades, which feeds an electric generator to **produce electricity**. Once the electricity is generated, it can be used, connected to the electrical grid or stored for future use. Wind farms with turbines as tall as skyscrapers are an increasingly **familiar sight** in many countries. The largest wind farm in the world, located in the Irish Sea just off the coast of the UK, is larger than the city of San Francisco.

Geothermal

If you've ever relaxed in a hot spring, you've used geothermal energy. In some places, such as Iceland, the heat is so close to the earth's surface it can be easily used as an energy source. In other places, holes must be drilled down through rocks to bring the hot underground water to the surface. Geothermal plants tend to have **low emissions** as long as the steam and water are pumped back into the underground reservoir.

Hydroelectric

One of the most **commercially developed** renewable energies, hydroelectric power relies on fast-moving water to **drive a turbine** and **generate electricity**. Hydroelectric power does not **cause pollution**, so is an **environmentally friendly** energy option. Utilising this energy source, however, has raised concerns because large hydroelectric plants can divert or reduce the natural flow of water that some animals and humans rely on.

Self-check 1

Complete the descriptions with words from the box. Two words are not used.

developed	emissions	energy	friendly	fuels
panels	sight	source	sustainable	turbine

1   Huge oil wells are a familiar _____ in eastern Saudi Arabia.

2   You may qualify for a rebate if you make your home more environmentally _____.

3   The country is well positioned to take advantage of solar as an energy
    _____.

4   Fossil _____, including coal, oil and natural gas, are currently the world's primary source of energy.

5   The price of solar _____ has gone down in recent years, allowing more people to install them in their home.

6   The goal of many manufacturers is to produce an everyday vehicle with low _____, or even none.

7   Many countries are working to lessen their dependence on oil and to utilise more renewable _____.

8   Electric cars will remain too expensive for most people unless they can be commercially _____ more cheaply.

Self-check 2

Unscramble the words to make sentences. There is one extra word in each set that is not needed.

1   the / drives / the / source / water / turbine

_____.

2   footprint / our / reduce / let's / carbon / sustainable

_____.

3   that / doesn't / pollution / environment / cause / factory

_____.

4   goal / energy / our / is / sustainable / emissions

_____.

5   for / footprint / three / cities / generate / we / electricity

_____.

6   natural / prefer / pollution / sources / of / energy / I

_____.

7   sight / electricity / factory / produces / the / no

_____.

Unit 31
Business

Aaron:	What are you working on?
Carolina:	Oh, I'm **drawing up a business plan**.
Aaron:	Really? For what?
Carolina:	I'm hoping to **go into business for myself**, so I'm just working through what I'd need to do to make that happen.
Aaron:	That's excellent. You'd be great at **running your own business**. What kind of business are you thinking of?
Carolina:	I'd like to have a food truck. I want to serve *pupusas*. They're a snack that are really popular in Honduras and El Salvador, and I think people here would love them.
Aaron:	Sounds interesting.
Carolina:	There's just so much to think about. For example, how do I **attract investors**? I don't really want to borrow a ton of money, but I do need **start-up capital**. I also still need to **do market research**. I have to make sure what I'm offering has a **competitive advantage**.
Aaron:	Well, it sounds like you're going about this the right away. I hope you can make it work.
Carolina:	Thanks.

Aaron:	One *pupusa*, please.
Carolina:	Aaron! Great to see you!
Aaron:	Wow, so this is your food truck? You did it!
Carolina:	Yeah, this is it. I started this up about three months ago.
Aaron:	Well, congratulations! What a fun way to **earn a living**. And to be your own boss.
Carolina:	Thanks. It's going well, but I worry about **going bankrupt** constantly. I have my regular customers, but I'm looking at ways to **boost sales**. Money has been tight.
Aaron:	Well, a lot of new businesses don't **make a profit** their first year. It takes time to **grow a business**.
Carolina:	Right. I'm thinking of **joining forces** with my cousin. She's really good at marketing, so I might see if she can give me some advice.
Aaron:	Maybe she has some ideas for **raising your profile**. I know that a lot of food trucks rely on social media to attract customers. Are you just serving *pupusas*?

Carolina:	So far that's it, but I'm thinking of **launching a new product**.
Aaron:	What kind of product?
Carolina:	My customers often want something a bit lighter, so I'm working on a grilled corn and pepper salad.
Aaron:	Yum!

Self-check I

Complete the sentences with words from the box. Two words are not used.

> boost   capital   competitive   draw   go
> launch   make   profile   raise   run

1   We will need about $10,000 in start-up _____ before we can open our shop.

2   They hope to _____ a new product that will appeal to the teen market.

3   Frida has some ideas on ways to _____ sales, and I think we should give them a try.

4   No one will take your ideas seriously unless you _____ up a business plan.

5   Your app idea is interesting, but what about it will give you a _____ advantage?

6   I worked in an office for a decade, and I'm now ready to _____ into business for myself.

7   After months of losses, July was the first month that we were able to _____ a profit.

8   If you want to _____ your own business well, always know where your money goes.

Self-check 2

Match the parts. Then use the phrases to complete the sentences.

join	a living
go	investors
earn	a business
raise	one's profile
grow	market research
attract	forces
do	bankrupt

1   I've been lucky with my business. I've been able to _____ doing what I love.

2   What's a good way to _____? Should we re-invest all of our profits?

3   I'm not good at asking for money, so what would be a good way to _____?

4   They have been losing money all year. I'm afraid they may _____ and close up.

5   It's important to _____, and one easy way to do that is by surveying people.

6   I'm good with people, but I may need to _____ with someone who's good with numbers.

7   It's no good if people don't know what a business is all about. Social media is one of the best ways to _____.

Unit 32
Money

Should Children Receive an Allowance?

Most people agree that it's good for children to learn about **financial literacy**. But not everyone agrees that an allowance is a good idea. We look at both sides of the issue.

Arguments for

Children need to learn about money, and the younger the better. The best way to do this is to actually **earn money**. An allowance does that. Then parents are not just 'giving' money for no reason.

It's essential that children have clear chores to do so they associate money with work. Parents can then provide a **set amount of money** as an allowance. If children don't do what is expected of them, they do not **receive an allowance**.

One way to teach the **value of money** is to break down the amount of the allowance. For example, insist that 10% is **donated to charity**. Then divide the remaining amount into thirds. One-third goes to long-term savings. Have them **put aside money for** college. They can do this by **opening a savings account** in a bank. One-third then goes to short-term savings. This is for something they want, but don't have enough money for yet, such as a new phone or a bicycle. The final one-third is for them to spend as they wish. This is their **pocket money**. They are free to use this money however they want.

Arguments against

It's important for children to have chores to do around the house, but it's not good for parents to give their children an allowance for these things. It can undermine the contributions that children make to their families. The children will believe that any chore they do always deserves a **monetary reward**. This is simply the wrong message. It also teaches them that working for money isn't always fun.

In addition, children may become less motivated to do their chores once they have **saved up money for** something. This could also make it a challenge for children to **manage their finances** later on.

Parents should always model **good financial habits**. The best way to do is to give (or not give) children money when they ask for it. That way the child has to explain what they want and why they need money for it. If a child wants to **splash out money on** something, they have to make a case for it. This helps the child to consider if the item is worth **spending money** on.

Self-check 1

Complete the paragraph with words from the box. Two words are not used.

account	allowance	amount	charity	financial
habits	pocket	spend	splurge	value

Everyone should develop good financial 1)_____ from an early age. This helps them later in life when they get a job and start saving for their future. But what is the best way to develop this 2)_____ literacy? Some experts think the best way is for children to receive a(n) 3)_____ from their parents. This is a set 4)_____ of money that is given to children, usually on a weekly basis. This money is often viewed by both parents and children as a kind of exchange. The children do certain chores around the house, and the money is for the children to spend as they wish. Some parents insist that children donate to 5)_____ or open a savings 6)_____ so they can grow their money. Whatever money is left is 7)_____ money for the children to spend as they wish. This all helps teach children the 8)_____ of money.

Self-check 2

Circle the correct words.

1 Some companies choose to provide their employees with monetary **rewards / gifts / cash** as an incentive to perform their jobs well.

2 I don't think it's smart to **pay / make / spend** money on things unless you have the cash on hand. It's a quick way to find yourself in debt.

3 I'm going to put **off / aside / down** money each month for my trip to Portugal next year. If I start now I don't think I'll miss the money much.

4 I will never understand how people can just **spend / splash / buy** out money on things like fancy clothes and meals.

5 It's not always easy for a student to **earn / pay / splurge** money while in college, but tutoring is one way to bring in some cash.

6 It's amazing how many young adults have no idea how to **manage / value / set aside** their finances. I think this is something that should be taught in high school.

7 Kevin dropped and broke his laptop, but he can't afford to replace it. He has to save **on / up / down** money to get a new one.

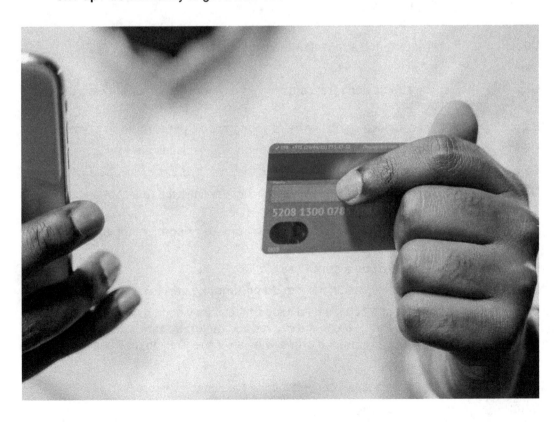

Unit 33
Crime

Ling:	You look upset. Is everything OK?
Cory:	Oh, I **got a ticket**. My first one.
Ling:	What for? Speeding?
Cory:	Yeah. Why couldn't they just **give me a warning**?
Ling:	Well, you did **break the law**.
Cory:	Are you serious? Speeding is such a **minor offense**. The police really should focus their efforts on more **dangerous criminals**. I wasn't going that fast, just a few kilometres over the speed limit.
Ling:	You know it's not safe to speed. What if you had hit someone?
Cory:	I guess.
Ling:	So what do you have to do? **Pay a fine**?
Cory:	Yeah, I have 30 days to pay. I might fight it, or just refuse to pay.
Ling:	I suggest that you just pay it and then forget about it. If you don't, they could **suspend your licence**.
Cory:	They wouldn't do that, would they?
Ling:	It's possible.

Uli:	What's with the recent **crime wave** in this city?
Sam:	What do you mean?
Uli:	The streets don't feel safe at night anymore. That's all they talk about on the news.
Sam:	Yeah, it does seem like more young people are **turning to crime**.
Uli:	I don't know the statistics, but I know car jackings are way up.
Sam:	I've heard that, too. Sometimes they steal your car in broad daylight.
Uli:	Those people need to **serve time**, or at the least the **repeat offenders** should.
Sam:	I don't know if I would **send someone to prison** for that, unless someone got hurt.
Uli:	There must be a better way.
Sam:	Maybe they should have to **do community service**.
Uli:	That's not a bad idea. I'd support that if they don't **have a criminal record**. But how can the city **reduce the crime rate**? I know that when someone **commits a crime**, they are more likely to do it again.
Sam:	Is that true?
Uli:	Maybe things will get better once the economy improves.
Sam:	I hope so.

Self-check 1

Unscramble the words to make sentences. There is one extra word in each set that is not needed.

1 law / she / break / the / didn't / crime

    _____.

2 a / serve / criminal / doesn't / he / record / have

    _____.

3 I / ticket / gotten / have / a / never / committed

    _____.

4 it's / to / rate / fine / the / important / crime / reduce

    _____.

5 him / a / police / the / gave / warning / wave

    _____.

6 paying / crime / more / are / people / to / turning

    _____.

7 is / offense / a / minor / stealing / law / not

    _____.

Self-check 2

Circle the correct words.

1 I don't know anyone who has **served / committed / gotten** a crime.
2 There is a dangerous **offender / repeater / criminal** on the loose in the city.
3 The judge **issued / sent / gave** the three men to prison.
4 If you park your car there, you may have to **pay / fight / serve** a fine.
5 Why do you think we're experiencing a crime **record / wave / rate**?
6 If someone robs a bank, they must **serve / make / pay** time.
7 The police have a right to **commit / send / suspend** your licence.
8 If you're a **criminal / repeat / community** offender, you might go to prison.

Unit 34
Behaviour

Interaction Styles

Interaction styles are based on observable **behaviour patterns.** They tell us the 'how' of human behaviour. Knowing the four interaction styles can help us to better understand **interpersonal conflicts.** They can also provide a map for greater flexibility in our interactions with others.

Chart-the-Course™ (Aim to get a desired result)

People of this style focus on knowing what to do and keeping everything on track. They prefer to enter a situation with an idea of what is going to happen. They identify a process to **accomplish a goal** and work to create and monitor a plan. The aim is not the plan itself, but to use it as a guide to move things along towards the **long-term goal**. Their decisions are based on analysing, outlining and foreseeing what needs to be done.

Behind-the-Scenes™ (Aim to get an integrated result)

People of this style work with the process to create a **positive outcome**. They see value in many contributions and look for input to make an **informed decision**. They accommodate different points of view and approach others with a calm style. Producing, defining and clarifying are all ways they support a group's process. They are patient with the time it takes to gain support and **reach a consensus**.

In-Charge™ (Aim to get an achievable result)

People of this style are focused on results, often **taking action** quickly. They have a driving energy with an intention to lead a group to the goal. They **make decisions** quickly to keep themselves and others **on task**, on target and on time. They hate to waste time. Executing actions, supervising and **mobilising resources** are all ways they get things accomplished. They notice right away what is not working in a situation.

Get-Things-Going™ (Aim to get an embraced result)

People of this style succeed in facilitator roles and aim to inspire others to move to action, assisting with the process. Their focus is on interaction, often with an expressive style. They have **intense energy**, enthusiasm and excitement. Exploring possibilities, **making preparations** and **sharing insights** are all ways they get people moving. They want decisions to be participative and enthusiastic.

Self-check 1

Match the parts. Then use the phrases to complete the definitions.

take	a consensus
make	insights
accomplish	resources
mobilise	action
reach	preparations
share	a goal

1 _____ = let others know your thoughts about something

2 _____ = come to an agreement on something

3 _____ = do things that help you prepare for something

4 _____ = complete the objective one set for oneself

5 _____ = bring together what's available and needed

6 _____ = do something decisively to get a desired result

Self-check 2

Circle the correct words.

1   My new assistant is reliable and hard-working, but he does have difficulty staying **on /
    in / at** task sometimes.

2   One quality that I admire in a manager is the ability to **take / find / make** decisions
    fairly and decisively.

3   We have a lot of options for who would be best for this role. Let's be sure we make
    an informed **goal / decision / conflict**.

4   The new student is exhibiting certain **behaviour / resource / action** patterns that we
    should keep an eye on.

5   The **action / outcome / interaction** styles of our two new employees are so different
    that we may not want to put them on the same team.

6   My parents continue to help me with money, but my long-term **goal / action /
    consensus** is to become financially independent.

7   The negotiations were long and difficult, but I'm happy to say we have a positive
    behaviour / outcome / resource that all parties are happy with.

8   The interpersonal **insights / outcomes / conflicts** between the two groups has
    sadly led to an increase in mistrust.

9   The new intern has an intense **energy / consensus / action** that not everyone finds
    to be a positive quality.

Unit 35
Advertising

Julia:	What do you think is the best way to **advertise a product** these days?
Mateo:	It depends. There are so many possibilities. I'd start by thinking about your **target audience**, and go from there.
Julia:	Well, we're hoping to sell to young professionals, as they have a lot of **buying power**.
Mateo:	What kind of **advertising budget** are we talking about?
Julia:	It's not much, I'm afraid, so we'll likely start with some **online adverts**.
Mateo:	That makes sense. Try to produce something that really grabs their attention.
Julia:	What kinds of adverts do you respond well to?
Mateo:	That's hard to say. I tend to buy things based on recommendations from people I trust, so maybe **word-of-mouth marketing**?
Julia:	I like that too. But it's not easy to make that happen.
Mateo:	Just remember, no matter how you advertise, consumers have a lot of choices these days.

Kai:	Why do you mute the TV every time there's a **commercial break**?
Sun-hee:	Oh, I can't stand listening to all the adverts on TV these days.
Kai:	I know what you mean. They can be pretty annoying.
Sun-hee:	It just seems there are more **TV adverts** than there used to be.
Kai:	You may be right. And I find most products don't **live up to the hype** anyway.
Sun-hee:	I just see the same commercials all the time. One might have a **catchy song** or something that's interesting the first time you hear it, but it **gets old** after a while.
Kai:	What would actually influence you to switch to a new brand?
Sun-hee:	I don't know. I have **brand loyalty** for certain things I guess, but not all. Sometimes I just go for what's cheapest, but I know that's not always a smart thing to do.
Kai:	Would a **celebrity endorsement** make any difference to you?
Sun-hee:	Not at all.
Kai:	What about **product placement** in films? Do you think that **has any effect on** sales?
Sun-hee:	It must for some people, or they wouldn't pay all that money to include it.

Self-check 1

Circle the correct words.

1   I really like that new TV **audience / placement / advert** with all of the singing chickens. It's one commercial I always stay and watch.

2   Our advertising **budget / audience / break** has been cut by over 50%. It's not going to be easy to get our message out.

3   A great advert should have a **brand / catchy / target** song, or something that helps you to remember the product.

4   It's not that expensive to advertise a **celebrity / product / placement** on the radio. You might want to consider that.

5   These **hype / online / brand** adverts are getting to be really annoying. Do you know if it's possible to block them?

6   That company also uses animals that 'talk' in their commercials. It's cute, but it's starting to **get / turn / make** old.

7   It's not clear if the commercials **took / had / made** an effect on sales in the American market.

8   To me, word-of-mouth **audience / marketing / power** is the most effective way to advertise something.

9   I bought that kitchen gadget they've been advertising on late-night TV, but it didn't **go / live / catch** up to the hype.

Self-check 2

Match the parts. Then use the phrases to complete the definitions.

brand	audience
product	power
target	placement
buying	endorsement
commercial	break
celebrity	loyalty

1 _____ = the group of people an ad is aimed at

2 _____ = the money a consumer is able to spend

3 _____ = an ad that features a famous person

4 _____ = showing a product in a TV show or film

5 _____ = an interruption of a TV or radio broadcast

6 _____ = the tendency to buy the same brand all the time

Unit 36
Art

Bryce Gallery

✕ •••

 taylorcg ✅ **Five stars!** Jul 18 at 3:00 pm

The new exhibit by **renowned artist** Andrea Loring at the Bryce Gallery is incredible. She **produces art** that really **speaks to her audience**. It was one of the most exciting exhibits I've seen in recent years. A **common thread** in her work is the use of colour and texture to display feelings of sorrow and loss. I hope more people can see her amazing work. I'd be interested in hearing what others thought of her work.

 marion124 ✅ **Huh?** Jul 18 at 4:00 pm

I recently saw her exhibit as well and I have to say I didn't **have an emotional reaction**. At all. I found it all a bit lifeless to be honest, so I am not sure what the fuss is all about. Maybe I just don't 'get' modern art. In fact, no one is my group liked it much, and we left disappointed. It's no wonder there has been a **decline in attendance** in museums and galleries over the years.

 karllutz ✅ **Not for me** Jul 18 at 4:00 pm

I have to agree with marion124. I **have a passion for** art, but this left me feeling empty inside. It seemed like something an art student would make (no offense). There are other exhibits at the Bryce that I would recommend over this one. Loring has clearly **developed a style** that is her own, but it's not one I really find appealing. To me, that's fine. Art is meant to encourage discussion.

 EMIKO8 ✅ **True talent** Jul 18 at 4:15 pm

Personally, I thought she really **demonstrated a mastery of** technique. She is clearly talented. Her paintings **are something to behold**. I wish I knew more about the motivation behind some of her art. I always like to hear an artist talk about their work so I can understand it.

 Artcritic101 ✅ **Go see it!** Jul 18 at 4:45 pm

I too was blown away by this exhibit. There was an **attention to detail** that is missing in many of the paintings that I've been lucky enough to see lately. Her piece *New Beginnings* is a **work of art**. She **deserves the attention** she has gotten for her work over the years.

 lucialopez22 ✅ **Meh!** Jul 18 at 5:00 pm

People say I have an eye for art, but I didn't care much for this. It just didn't **leave a lasting impression** on me. But art is a **matter of taste**. It's not surprising that some people like her work, and other don't. Loring would probably be the first person to say that's fine with her!

Self-check 1

Circle the correct word. Then use the phrases to complete the sentences.

> work **by / of / to** art
> **idea / choice / matter** of taste
> **make / ensure / deserve** the attention
> attention **for / to / of** detail
> (be) something to **hold / holder / behold**
> leave a **lasting / later / forever** impression

1 The _____ in this sculpture is incredible.

2 The dance performance didn't _____ on me

3 People love that film, but not me. It's just a(n) _____.

4 Leonardo's drawings are truly _____.

5 The *Mona Lisa* is arguably the most famous _____ in the world.

6 Eleanor and Marco's film is cool. They _____ they've received.

Self-check 2

Each sentence has an error. Replace the ~~crossed out~~ word.

1 Anyone can ~~taste~~ _____ art, so does that make everyone an artist?

2 He is a ~~high~~ _____ artist today, but people ignored his work during his lifetime.

3 The graffiti art she creates really ~~talks~~ _____ to her audience in a meaningful way.

4 I had an emotional ~~feedback~~ _____ to that poetry reading. It made me cry.

5 The brushstrokes in this painting ~~determine~~ _____ a mastery that few possess.

6 There has been a ~~deterioration~~ _____ in attendance in museums and galleries.

7 She has a passion ~~of~~ _____ dance, and hopes to study performing arts.

8 I like his artwork, but he needs to ~~grow~~ _____ a style that is his own.

9 She grew up poor, so poverty is a common ~~idea~~ _____ in her work.

Unit 37
Exploration

Tracy:	Are you working on your essay?
Quinn:	I am. I decided to write about exploration.
Tracy:	That's an interesting topic. I've always been fascinated by the people who travelled the old overland **trade routes** between Europe and Asia. You know - the **spice trade**.
Quinn:	Me too, but I'm writing more about the people who explored the oceans and seas.
Tracy:	Like Ferdinand Magellan?
Quinn:	Exactly. Magellan was the first person to **circle the globe.** Well, his men did. Magellan died before completing the journey. Magellan was from Portugal, but King Charles I of Spain **sponsored the expedition** in 1519.
Tracy:	That's interesting. Magellan was the first European to land in the Philippines if I remember correctly.
Quinn:	Right. That's actually where he died. I'm also writing about James Cook, who **extensively explored** the Pacific in the late 1700s. He **led** three **expeditions** there. He made many **significant discoveries**, including being the first European to visit Hawaii.
Tracy:	Didn't he die there?
Quinn:	Sadly, yes. He was killed there on this third visit to the Pacific.

Marco:	Do you think **space tourism** will ever be possible for the average person?
Jon:	I'm not sure. I haven't really thought about it.
Marco:	The technology is certainly there, but it's just so expensive.
Jon:	I know there are several private companies that now **offer flights**, but you would have to be a millionaire to afford one.
Marco:	It seems that the **private sector** is way ahead of a lot of governments in this regard.
Jon:	So would you ever take a trip to **outer space**?
Marco:	Of course! I'd **jump at the opportunity**. What kid hasn't dreamed of going to space, and experiencing **zero gravity**. Or being one of the first humans to colonise Mars.
Jon:	It's never been a **lifelong dream** of mine, but I can understand the appeal.
Marco:	Anyone would have to **undergo training,** and I imagine there would be all sorts of tests to determine if you could handle the trip, both physically and emotionally.
Jon:	I can tell you right now I wouldn't be able to pass all those tests!

Self-check 1

Complete the sentences with words from the box. Two words are not used.

> discovery   dream   globe   outer   sector   space
>
> spice   trade   training   zero

1 It's likely that _____ tourism will be something that only the rich will get to experience.

2 Early explorers followed _____ routes that had been established by their predecessors.

3 One of the perks of being an astronaut is that they get to float around in _____ gravity.

4 It has always been a lifelong _____ of mine to stand on the Great Wall of China.

5 I think the best thing about a trip to _____ space would be looking back at the Earth.

6 The private _____ is leading the push to travel to and eventually colonise Mars.

7 Finding life on another planet or moon would be a very significant _____.

8 The _____ trade made many nations along its routes very wealthy.

Self-check 2

Unscramble the words to make sentences. There is one extra word in each set that is not needed.

1 Antarctica / chance / airline / to / offers / flights / no

   _____.

2 to / lead / an / will / explore / expedition / she / the Amazon

   _____.

3 training / must / in Kazakhstan / trade / undergo / she

   _____.

4 he / by sailboat / space / the / globe / circle / plans to

   _____.

5 haven't / discovered / extensively / been / the islands / explored

   _____.

6 opportunity / for / jumped / at / they / the

   _____.

7 he'll / to / the Sahara / an / expedition / exploration / sponsor

   _____.

Unit 38
Politics

FAQs – British Politics Explained

For residents and visitors alike, politics in the UK can be confusing **at first glance**. This quick guide to some frequently asked questions is meant to help demystify British politics.

What type of government is the UK?

The UK is a constitutional monarchy, meaning it is governed by a king or a queen. It is largely a **ceremonial role**. It involves representing the country at home and abroad, hosting a visiting **head of state**, and opening new sessions of parliament. The UK is also a parliamentary democracy.

What exactly is parliament?

Parliament consists of two chambers – the House of Commons and the House of Lords. Those in the House of Commons are directly elected. Their main role is to **debate issues** and **make laws.** Those in the House of Lords **serve for life** and are mostly appointed by the government. Their main role is to **vote on legislation** that was passed by the House of Commons.

Is the UK a two-party system?

British politics has recently been dominated by two parties The Labour Party is more left-wing and Conservative Party is more right-wing. There are also many smaller parties, such as the Green Party and the Liberal Democrats.

How does the voting system work?

The **political party** that wins the most votes **wins the election**. They need to have a majority to **form a government**. Without a majority, there is something called a 'hung parliament'. When this happens, a larger party and a smaller party come together to **form a coalition**.

Do people vote for the prime minister?

Voters do not elect the prime minister directly. Rather, they vote to **elect a candidate** that represents a particular party. The leader of the party that wins the most seats is then asked by the king or queen to form a government. This person then becomes prime minister.

When does an election take place?

An election happens at least every five years. However, the government can **call an election** at any time. This happens when the prime minister asks the king or queen to **dissolve parliament**. An election must then take place within weeks. It is customary to **hold an election** on a Thursday.

Self-check 1

Complete the sentences with words from the box. Two words are not used.

debate	dissolve	elect	form	hold
increase	pass	serve	vote	win

1   The winner of the election now needs to _____ a government before it can rule.

2   The new leader was able to _____ the election with 51% of the vote.

3   The legislature needs to _____ issues before it can pass any laws.

4   I think we can agree that it's necessary to _____ parliament once again.

5   I hope we can _____ a candidate that will listen to the will of the people.

6   The United States can _____ an election for president only every four years.

7   The judges _____ for life, so they never have to deal with elections.

8   The lawmakers plan to _____ on legislation that will protect our privacy.

Self-check 2

Circle the correct words.

1   The new queen has a mostly ceremonial **place / role / state**.

2   The prime minister plans to **make / call / vote** an election next month.

3   The current **head / leader / minister** of state has no political experience.

4   Which **election / candidate / political** party do most people in your country belong to?

5   At first **look / glance / view** it seems there is no real difference in these candidates.

6   It's their responsibility to **do / make / elect** laws that improve people's lives.

7   Before she can rule, she needs to **form / take / rule** a coalition with another party.

Unit 39
Humour

Ollie:	Well, that was an interesting film.
Erika:	Didn't you like it?
Ollie:	I don't know … I thought it was a comedy, but I never **laughed out loud** once.
Erika:	You didn't think it was funny at all?
Ollie:	I think whatever humour there was just **fell flat**. It just wasn't for me.
Erika:	Wow, I totally loved it. The two main actors are mostly in dramas, but I think they **have a knack for** comedy.
Ollie:	Huh. Your **sense of humour** clearly is very different from mine.
Erika:	Perhaps. I found it **hysterically funny** to be honest.
Ollie:	Really?
Erika:	Yeah, I mean I **burst out laughing** when the kids asked their parents for money. I didn't see that coming.
Ollie:	I'm more used to **physical comedy** I guess. There just wasn't that much action or anything to keep me interested. They just talked a lot.
Erika:	There was a lot of **dry humour**, I suppose, but that's not for everyone.

Ana:	Have you met Ken yet? He started in Accounting the other day.
Will:	No, I haven't. What's he like?
Ana:	Well, I spoke to him when we were both getting coffee the other morning. He was **doing an impression of** his boss.
Will:	What? That's not appropriate.
Ana:	I know. Then he told an **offensive joke**.
Will:	No! What did you do?
Ana:	I just let out a **forced laugh** and walked away. I should have told him that it wasn't cool to joke about people like that, but I was just so shocked.
Will:	Maybe he was just nervous and trying to get people to like him.
Ana:	I can understand him trying to **get a laugh**, but he's going about it the wrong way. No one should tell ever tell a joke that's **in poor taste**, and certainly not at work.
Will:	I agree. He reminds me of that guy that used to work here. Do you remember Rick?
Ana:	Rick … yeah … oh, he would **do anything for a laugh**.
Will:	Do you remember when he decided to **pull a prank** on Melissa? He wanted to put a rubber snake on her chair to scare her, but we talked him out of it.
Ana:	I do remember that. We didn't think it was funny.

Self-check 1

Circle the correct words.

1   Mandy always has to be the centre of attention. She'll do anything to **get / make / take** a laugh.

2   Alexander is a pretty funny guy. He can **work / make / do** an impression of Mr Livingston that's hilarious.

3   I think the most important quality to have in a partner is a sense of **laughter / comedy / humour**.

4   Nate told this long joke about an old farmer and three cows today, but it **fell / went / dropped** flat.

5   Ashley got in a lot of trouble because she posted a video that was **to / in / by** poor taste. She has since taken it down.

6   Charlie has a **way / knack / laugh** for comedy, and dreams of moving to Hollywood to become a screenwriter.

7   Mikhail and his brother are a lot of fun to be around. They will do anything for **funny / humour / a laugh**.

8   All the kids at the birthday party burst **out / up / through** laughing when the clown walked into the giant cake.

Self-check 2

Each sentence has an error. Replace the ~~crossed out~~ word.

1   When Ian told his joke, Dory let out a ~~forceful~~ _____ laugh.

2   The new play that we saw was ~~hysterical~~ _____ funny.

3   I want to pull a ~~joke~~ _____ on my next-door neighbours.

4   Nico is funny, but he has a dry ~~prank~~ _____.

5   Why did Sheila tell such an offensive ~~laugh~~ _____?

6   Lacy and Jess are masters of ~~bodily~~ _____ comedy.

7   Paulo ~~joked~~ _____ out loud when he read that story.

Unit 40
Globalisation

Our Global World

We live in a **global village**, and that is due to globalisation, defined as 'the increase in the flow of goods, services, capital, people and ideas across international borders'. This has undoubtedly brought benefits to our modern life, but it is not without drawbacks. In this essay, I will discuss both the advantages and disadvantages of globalisation in the 21st century.

Globalisation has influenced the world's economy in many positive ways. It has certainly led to **greater economic growth** worldwide. It makes more **goods and services** available to more people, usually at lower prices. These practices have given nations access to a wider labour pool. **Developed countries** may **outsource production** to **developing countries** with a lower cost of living, providing jobs in the process. This allows developing countries to reduce the costs of good and services, which can then be passed onto consumers.

At the same time, developing countries may also import high-skilled workers, which can help to **jumpstart their economies**. New equipment, technologies and management skills can all be beneficial for the local job market. Through this all there is the need for increased cooperation. In our globalised world, all nations must work together. This can help to reduce potential conflicts around the world.

However, while **free trade** can be beneficial, this can be a disadvantage to individual countries, companies and workers. Small- and medium-sized businesses may have to close down if they are unable to compete or gain access to resources. As a result, it has led to unemployment and exploitation. Some feel that rich countries just get richer, **at the expense of** poorer nations. In other words, there has merely been a re-distribution of wealth.

Globalisation has caused some governments to implement policies that aim to protect against **foreign competition**. They may implement **trade barriers**, form trading blocs or adopt other protectionist policies. In fact, some economists believe that globalisation has not actually created more jobs globally. Instead, they argue that it has simply shifted employment opportunities from more developed countries to less developed ones. In addition, the **global economy** has created many environmental challenges, including increased pollution and the exploitation of local resources. This is true for both **emerging economies** and more **mature markets**.

In conclusion, there is no doubt that globalisation is here to stay. It will continue to **play a role** in our modern world, but we should not ignore the negative impact this can have. Governments and companies must take appropriate but fair steps so they can fully engage in a free trade economy around the world.

Self-check I

Circle the correct words.

1   What strategies do corporations utilise to help them enter **old / mature / settled** markets?

2   Why don't governments do more to advance the idea of **free / welcome / permitted** trade?

3   If you want to **do / make / play** a role in shaping the agreement, put forth some ideas.

4   A **total / global / universal** village refers to the entire world becoming more connected.

5   **Developed / progressed / grown** countries don't contribute enough to combat climate change.

6   The new trade **hurdles / barriers / fences** were criticised by the global community.

7   The failure of nations to help others could cost the global **economy / savings / wealth** billions.

8   The tax on imports is meant to protect us from **alien / imported / foreign** competition.

Self-check 2

Unscramble the words to make sentences.

1 tax / on / there's / and / services / a / goods

    _____.

2 is / countries / this / of / developing / list / a

    _____.

3 led / to / investment / growth / the / economic / greater

    _____.

4 jumpstart / the / money / should / economy / that

    _____.

5 no / an / we / economy / emerging / are / longer

    _____.

6 the / environment / expense / got / at / rich / of / the / they

    _____.

7 production / our / outsource / wants / to / company

    _____.

Self-check
Answers

Unit 1

Self-check 1

1 make; 2 paths; 3 casual; 4 close; 5 friends; 6 particularly; 7 develop

Self-check 2

1 repair; 2 speaking; 3 destroy; 4 exceptionally; 5 famously; 6 divulge; 7 friendly; 8 true

Unit 2

Self-check 1

1 members; 2 single; 3 extended; 4 roof; 5 related; 6 nuclear; 7 blended; 8 divorced

Self-check 2

1 breadwinner; 2 widow; 3 get; 4 traditional; 5 bring; 6 adopted; 7 blood

Unit 3

Self-check 1

1 I took a selfie with my phone. 2 It's easy to check your messages.
3 Gia is addicted to social media. 4 Omar is very active on social media.
5 You should manage your settings. 6 Emiko never comments on threads.

Self-check 2

1 viral; 2 post; 3 request; 4 upload; 5 link; 6 add; 7 site; 8 trending

Unit 4

Self-check 1

1 middle-class neighbourhood; 2 put down a deposit; 3 first-time buyer;
4 a home of my own; 5 all the comforts of home; 6 in the suburbs

Self-check 2

1 modest; 2 put down; 3 childhood; 4 pay; 5 forever; 6 head; 7 single-family; 8 truly; 9 starter

English Collocations in Context

Unit 5

Self-check 1
1 college; 2 off; 3 program; 4 for; 5 receive; 6 fees; 7 university; 8 out

Self-check 2
1 attend; 2 live; 3 hit; 4 pay off; 5 graduate; 6 declare; 7 take; 8 sit for

Unit 6

Self-check 1
1 develop good eating habits; 2 work up an appetite; 3 make a shopping list;
4 grab a bite to eat; 5 satisfy your sweet tooth; 6 have a balanced diet;
7 shop on an empty stomach; 8 cook from scratch

Self-check 2
1 quick; 2 fast; 3 check; 4 home-cooked; 5 junk; 6 go-to; 7 packaged; 8 ready-made

Unit 7

Self-check 1
1 has the same eyes; 2 has shoulder-length hair; 3 is in his early 20s; 4 has red hair;
5 is in good shape; 6 is fashionably dressed; 7 has a full head of hair

Self-check 2
1 slim; 2 youthful; 3 young; 4 bald; 5 broad; 6 strongly; 7 athletic; 8 old

Unit 8

Self-check 1
1 travel off season; 2 go abroad; 3 score a deal; 4 plan a trip; 5 take in the sights;
6 book a flight; 7 obtain a visa

Self-check 2
1 holiday; 2 take; 3 track; 4 reserve; 5 travel; 6 on; 7 inclusive; 8 at

Unit 9

Self-check 1
1 do; 2 go; 3 grab; 4 go for; 5 hang out; 6 develop; 7 stream

Self-check 2
1 fun; 2 outdoor; 3 playing; 4 have; 5 get; 6 have; 7 gets; 8 thoroughly

Unit 10

Self-check 1
1 slashes prices; 2 attracts customers; 3 is in the black; 4 hits the shops; 5 picks up a bargain; 6 goes on a shopping spree

Self-check 2
1 store; 2 -bottom; 3 in; 4 bargain-; 5 shopping; 6 top-; 7 discounts; 8 season; 9 -hard

Unit 11

Self-check 1
1 natural; 2 at; 3 born; 4 lack; 5 for; 6 with; 7 mastery; 8 athletic

Self-check 2
1 He Is a natural. 2 She possesses skills in business. 3 He acquires skills through practice. 4 Driving is a very practical skill. 5 They demonstrate raw talent in tennis. 6 She has the ability to do the job. 7 Languages are not his strong suit.

Unit 12

Self-check 1
1 blue; 2 weather; 3 pouring; 4 bright; 5 fine; 6 cold; 7 changeable; 8 heat

Self-check 2
1 weather; 2 light; 3 under; 4 gloomy; 5 cloud; 6 extreme; 7 gentle
1 traits; 2 shy; 3 numbers; 4 dominant; 5 overly; 6 mind; 7 organised; 8 attitude

Unit 13

Self-check 1
1 soft-spoken; 2 quick-tempered; 3 easy-going; 4 strong-willed; 5 closed-minded;
6 hard-working; 7 self-reliant

Self-check 2
1 traits; 2 shy; 3 numbers; 4 dominant; 5 overly; 6 mind; 7 organised; 8 attitude

Unit 14

Self-check 1
1 rainforest; 2 cascade; 3 range; 4 volcano; 5 landscape; 6 wonder; 7 system; 8 life

Self-check 2
1 populated; 2 reach; 3 natural; 4 active; 5 fauna; 6 climb; 7 natural

Unit 15

Self-check 1
1 I am not a morning person. 2 My daily routine is very boring. 3 I like to get an early start.
4 I don't have a typical day. 5 He hates to take out the rubbish. 6 She does her makeup in five
minutes. 7 I enjoy curling up with a good book. 8 There are a million and one things to do

Self-check 2
1 chores; 2 shower; 3 nap; 4 laundry; 5 errands; 6 teeth; 7 dressed; 8 takeaway

Unit 16

Self-check 1
1 make; 2 prospects; 3 nine-to-five; 4 day-to-day; 5 apply for; 6 position; 7 from;
8 flexible

Self-check 2
1 job; 2 work; 3 redundant; 4 living; 5 job; 6 job; 7 follow

Unit 17

Self-check 1

1 asleep; 2 to sleep; 3 back; 4 night's; 5 awake; 6 grab; 7 turning

Self-check 2

1 She had a bad dream. 2 He didn't get a wink of sleep. 3 After my nap I was good as new.
4 She forgot to set her alarm. 5 I always hit the snooze button. 6 We feel dead to the world.
7 I need to recharge my batteries. 8 I got up at the crack of dawn.

Unit 18

Self-check 1

1 reach; 2 quit; 3 establish; 4 maintain; 5 keep; 6 learn; 7 practise; 8 do

Self-check 2

1 healthy; 2 mental; 3 of; 4 healthy; 5 nurture; 6 well-being; 7 pains; 8 physical

Unit 19

Self-check 1

1 deeply hurt; 2 absolutely thrilled; 3 hopelessly confused; 4 eternally grateful;
5 terribly sad; 6 pleasantly surprised; 7 perfectly normal; 8 wildly optimistic

Self-check 2

1 Peter is utterly amazed by his grade. 2 Valerie is totally serious about quitting.
3 The experience raises my self-esteem. 4 I have a nagging feeling about this. 5 Wendy was filled with fear. 6 Your email took me by surprise. 7 Jacqueline was scared to death.

Unit 20

Self-check 1

1 dress the part; 2 take pride in one's appearance; 3 be out of fashion; 4 mix and match;
5 have an eye for fashion; 6 buy off the rack

Self-check 2

1 attire; 2 Proper; 3 latest; 4 whole; 5 neutral; 6 designer; 7 forward; 8 sense; 9 item

English Collocations in Context

Unit 21

Self-check 1
1 keep; **2** spent; **3** incredibly; **4** spare; **5** minute; **6** spend; **7** demanding

Self-check 2
1 had; **2** ran; **3** wasted; **4** took; **5** on; **6** extra; **7** pressed; **8** made

Unit 22

Self-check 1
1 inside; **2** grab; **3** tabloid; **4** check; **5** fake; **6** fair; **7** run; **8** flesh

Self-check 2
1 go on; **2** made up; **3** confirm; **4** leaked; **5** report on; **6** check

Unit 23

Self-check 1
1 have a cool vibe; **2** leave a tip; **3** look over the menu; **4** ask for the bill;
5 split a dessert; **6** pick up the tab

Self-check 2
1 fine; **2** menu; **3** daily; **4** options; **5** separate; **6** distance; **7** water; **8** casual; **9** catch

Unit 24

Self-check 1
1 rising temperatures; **2** habitat loss; **3** urban sprawl; **4** endangered species;
5 farming practices; **6** food waste

Self-check 2
1 insecurity; **2** global; **3** crisis; **4** pass; **5** at; **6** consequences; **7** climate; **8** reach; **9** on

Unit 25

Self-check 1
1 have a lot in common; 2 go on a date; 3 meet by chance; 4 have chemistry;
5 make a commitment; 6 see eye to eye

Self-check 2
1 at; 2 healthy; 3 long; 4 double; 5 celebrate; 6 through; 7 on; 8 seeing; 9 date

Unit 26

Self-check 1
1 give; 2 make; 3 communicate; 4 project; 5 make; 6 tell; 7 convey; 8 engage

Self-check 2
1 communication; 2 facial; 3 language; 4 look; 5 communicator; 6 sign; 7 face-to-face

Unit 27

Self-check 1
1 I need to lose weight. 2 That company has great power. 3 Limit the size of the group.
4 A million is a huge number. 5 I want to watch my weight. 6 That's a considerable number.
7 They always make huge profits.

Self-check 2
1 big mistake; 2 big accomplishment; 3 great admiration; 4 ideal weight; 5 strong argument;
6 large proportion; 7 high in fat; 8 corporate giant

Unit 28

Self-check 1
1 national; 2 celebrate; 3 express; 4 thanks; 5 exchange; 6 do; 7 make; 8 hold

Self-check 2
1 offer; 2 seek; 3 pay; 4 marks; 5 cause; 6 atmosphere; 7 serves

Unit 29

Self-check 1

1 cutting-edge technology; 2 back up my files; 3 adopt technology; 4 light years ahead;
5 control remotely; 6 not rocket science

Self-check 2

1 user-; 2 -savvy; 3 -speed; 4 electronic; 5 technologies; 6 technological;
7 sense; 8 receive; 9 in

Unit 30

Self-check 1

1 sight; 2 friendly; 3 source; 4 fuels; 5 panels; 6 emissions; 7 energy; 8 developed

Self-check 2

1 The water drives the turbine. 2 Let's reduce our carbon footprint. 3 That factory doesn't
cause pollution. 4 Our goal is sustainable energy. 5 We generate electricity for three
cities. 6 I prefer natural sources of energy. 7 The factory produces no electricity.

Unit 31

Self-check 1

1 capital; 2 launch; 3 boost; 4 draw; 5 competitive; 6 go; 7 make; 8 run

Self-check 2

1 earn a living; 2 grow a business; 3 attract investors; 4 go bankrupt;
5 do market research; 6 join forces; 7 raise one's profile

Unit 32

Self-check 1

1 habits; 2 financial; 3 allowance; 4 amount; 5 charity; 6 account; 7 pocket; 8 value

Self-check 2

1 rewards; 2 spend; 3 aside; 4 splash; 5 earn; 6 manage; 7 up

Unit 33

Self-check 1

1 She didn't break the law. 2 He doesn't have a criminal record. 3 I have never gotten a ticket. 4 It's important to reduce the crime rate. 5 The police gave him a warning.
6 More people are turning to crime. 7 Stealing is not a minor offense.

Self-check 2

1 committed; 2 criminal; 3 sent; 4 pay; 5 wave; 6 serve; 7 suspend; 8 repeat

Unit 34

Self-check 1

1 share insights; 2 reach a consensus; 3 make preparations; 4 reach a goal;
5 mobilise resources; 6 take action

Self-check 2

1 on; 2 make; 3 decision; 4 behaviour; 5 interaction; 6 goal; 7 outcome; 8 conflicts;
9 energy

Unit 35

Self-check 1

1 advert; 2 budget; 3 catchy; 4 product; 5 online; 6 get; 7 had; 8 marketing; 9 live

Self-check 2

1 target audience; 2 buying power; 3 celebrity endorsement; 4 product placement;
5 commercial break; 6 brand loyalty

Unit 36

Self-check 1

1 attention to detail; 2 leave a lasting impression; 3 matter of taste; 4 something to behold;
5 work of art; 6 deserve the attention

Self-check 2

1 produce; 2 renowned; 3 speaks; 4 reaction; 5 demonstrate; 6 decline; 7 for;
8 develop; 9 thread

Unit 37

Self-check 1

1 space; 2 trade; 3 zero; 4 dream; 5 outer; 6 sector; 7 discovery; 8 spice

Self-check 2

1 No airline offers flights to Antarctica. 2 She will lead an expedition to the Amazon.
3 She must undergo training in Kazakhstan. 4 He plans to circle the globe by sailboat.
5 The islands haven't been extensively explored. *or* The islands haven't been explored
extensively. 6 They jumped at the opportunity. 7 He'll sponsor an expedition to the Sahara.

Unit 38

Self-check 1

1 form; 2 win; 3 debate; 4 dissolve; 5 elect; 6 hold; 7 serve; 8 vote

Self-check 2

1 role; 2 call; 3 head; 4 political; 5 glance; 6 make; 7 form

Unit 39

Self-check 1

1 get; 2 do; 3 humour; 4 fell; 5 in; 6 knack; 7 a laugh; 8 out

Self-check 2

1 forced; 2 hysterically; 3 prank; 4 humour; 5 joke; 6 physical; 7 laughed

Unit 40

Self-check 1

1 mature; 2 free; 3 play; 4 global; 5 developed; 6 barriers; 7 economy; 8 foreign

Self-check 2

1 There's a tax on goods and services. 2 This is a list of developing countries.
3 The investment led to greater economic growth. 4 That money should jumpstart the
economy. 5 We are no longer an emerging economy. 6 They got rich at the expense of the
environment. 7 Our company wants to outsource production.

Appendix
Collocation expansion

This section features additional collocations related to each unit's topic. These are not practised in the book, but it's a good idea to look over these collocations as well. All collocations are indexed on pages 141–161.

Unit 1

mutual / social acquaintance; **good / dear / lifelong / trusted** friend; **childhood / old / family / long-lost** friend; **bunch / group / network** of friends; **bonds / offer / gesture / token** of friendship; **become / stay / remain** friends; be on **good / bad / friendly** terms with someone; **form / strike up / build / nurture / renew** a friendship; **wreck / spoil / ruin** a friendship; **seek / enjoy** someone's company; **keep / share / reveal** a secret; **genuinely / extremely** friendly; not be **exactly / especially** friendly

Unit 2

birth **mother / parents**; adoptive **mother / father / parents**; foster **child / children / mother / father / parents**; **biological / close-knit / tight** family; family **gathering / reunion / dynamics / unit**; be **family / flesh and blood**; **birth / divorce** rate; get **engaged / married** to someone; get **separated / divorced** from someone; **raise / bring up** a child; take after one's **mother / father**; live with one's **partner / spouse / significant other**; have a child **on one's own / out of wedlock**

Unit 3

social media **activity / platform / trends / troll / influencer**; like **a post / a photo / a page / a video / an image / a meme / a GIF**; share **a post / a photo / a page / a video / an image / a meme / a GIF**; upload **a post / a photo / a page / a video / an image / a meme / a GIF**; post **a link / a message / an update / a photo / a video / an image**; go **online / on the internet**; **friend / follow / unfriend** someone; update one's **status / profile**; attach a **file / document / photo**; **accept / refuse** a friend request; manage your **devices / accounts**; **private / direct / instant** message; virtual **event / learning / network**

Unit 4

spacious / cosy / self-contained / furnished flat; **affordable / comfortable / family** home; **semi-detached / three-bedroom / two-bed one-bath** home; **second / holiday / dream** home; **loving / caring / happy** home; home **life / situation / environment**; **permanent / temporary** address; **friendly / close / next-door** neighbour; **nice / respectable / run-down / surrounding** neighbourhood; **leave / come / make one's way / return** home; **buy / sell / own / let / sublet / take** a flat; **get a / take out a / pay off one's** mortgage; block of **apartments / flats**

Unit 5

secondary / high-school / higher / tertiary / university education; **trade / language / co-ed / private / public** school; **four-year / community / technical** college; **face-to-face / online / hybrid / vocational / distance-learning** course; **graduate / post-graduate** studies; **associate's / bachelor's / master's / PhD** degree; **student / academic / social** life; **under-graduate / graduate / post-graduate** student; receive **a grant / an award**; attend **class / a tutorial / a module**; **finish / complete / graduate from** high school; **study for / take / re-take / pass / fail** an exam; **learn / know** something by heart

Unit 6

simple / cooked / tinned / frozen / leftover food; **nutritious / gourmet / quality / organic** food; **main / side / tasty / delicious / mouth-watering** dish; **follow a / try a new / go on a** diet; **follow / try out / stick to** a recipe; **have / try / take** a bite; **pick at / play with** one's food; **order / pick up** take-away; **check / ask for / look at / choose from** the menu; **pay / foot / settle** the bill; **big / messy / fussy / picky** eater; **take / place / call in** an order; have a **taste / meal / snack**; **welcome / celebratory / farewell** dinner; be dying of **hunger / thirst**

Unit 7

be in one's **early / mid / late** 30s; look **one's / young for one's / old for one's** age; have **dark / light / blond / grey / dyed** hair; have **long / short / thinning** hair; have **dark / brown / green / blue / hazel** eyes; have a **lovely / fair** complexion; be **light- / fair- / dark-**skinned; have a **pretty / handsome / round / plain** face; be in **excellent / poor / terrible** shape; be **slightly / somewhat / a bit** overweight; be **nicely / poorly / casually / well-**dressed; **closely / greatly / strongly** resemble someone; bear **a striking / an uncanny** resemblance to someone

Unit 8

holiday / leisure / business travel; domestic / international / overseas / foreign travel; air / rail / bus / train travel; travel documents / plans / arrangements / deal; affordable / exotic / holiday / travel / far-off destination; guided / self-guided / package / group tour; travel abroad / on business / the world; take / have / go on a holiday; make a booking / reservation; book a ticket / room / hotel / day trip; take / go on a tour; tourist trap / hot spot; economy / business / second / first class; charter / long-haul flight; low-cost carrier / airline

Unit 9

leisure time / activities; have / get / meet for / catch up over a coffee; have / get / meet for / go out for lunch; spend one's free time / weekends / days off; spend time together / with someone / alone; play a game / a sport / a musical instrument; do karaoke / karate / tae kwon do; go running / climbing / shopping; go for a walk / bike ride / drive / run; go on a picnic / an adventure; have a barbecue / party / small get-together; download / watch a movie; take up a new hobby / sport; have a blast / good time; develop a passion for something

Unit 10

find / snap up a bargain; get / find a good deal; pay a lower / the full price; ask for / receive a discount; ask for / receive a refund; return / exchange an item; use a coupon / voucher / gift card / discount code; generous / massive / huge discount; late-night / last-minute / one-stop / online / window shopping; department / chain / discount / independent / family-owned store; high-street / wholesale / retail / corner shop; special sale / discount / promotion; big-ticket / must-have / luxury item; smart / impulse buy; do the shopping

Unit 11

communication / practical / personal / life skills; have / display / lack / master skills; musical / artistic / proven ability; demonstrate / lose one's ability; enormous / considerable / genuine / tremendous / major / innate / hidden talent; have / possess / display / lack talent; be bad / terrible at something; have an eye / a nose for something; do something to the best of one's ability; do something with one's eyes closed

Unit 12

great / lovely / beautiful weather; nasty / terrible / awful weather; severe / unpredictable weather; in spring / summer / fall / winter; dry / wet / rainy season; low / high / extreme temperatures; light / steady / heavy / torrential rain; light / deep / heavy snow; light / strong / brisk / high wind; a spell of good / bad weather; a cold / warm spell; a change in temperature / the weather; be hit by a storm / snowstorm

Unit 13

colourful / outgoing / larger-than-life / unique personality; distinct / abrasive / strong / complex personality; show / reveal / express / reflect one's personality; personality type / trait / quirk; caring / liberal / mature attitude; uncaring / dismissive / elitist attitude; have a rational / logical / creative mind; self-confident / disciplined / absorbed / assured / centered; overly critical / dramatic / sensitive; open- / broad- / narrow-minded; big- / hot- / level-headed; street / book smart; a people / an ideas person

Unit 14

northern / southern / eastern / western hemisphere; temperate / equatorial / tropical / polar climate; temperate / equatorial / tropical / polar region; temperate / equatorial / tropical / polar zone; high / low latitudes; be at a latitude / longitude of; high / low pressure; high / low / strong / rising tide; marine environment / ecosystem; arid desert / land / conditions; volcanic / deep / shallow crater; native / marine / rich flora; native / marine / diverse fauna; wildlife habitat / park / reserve / sanctuary / rehabilitation; cross / straddle the equator

Unit 15

morning / afternoon / evening / weekday routine; typical morning / afternoon / evening / weekday; go to class / work / the office / bed / sleep; take a bath / a break / some rest; order in / food / lunch / dinner; do housework / the cleaning / the cooking / the dishes / the washing-up; have coffee / tea / breakfast / dinner; water the plants / garden / lawn; make coffee / breakfast / lunch / dinner / the bed; take out the trash / garbage / recycling; wash / dry / fold / iron / put away the clothes; wash / dry / comb / brush one's hair; a fixed / flexible schedule; force / creature of habit

Unit 16

job **perks / security / satisfaction**; working **conditions / environment**; **desk / low-paid / well-paid / lucrative / dream** job; **steady / temporary / flexible / blue-collar / white-collar** job; **long / distinguished / promising / successful** career; **work / hands-on / on-the-job** experience; **hard / challenging / demanding / rewarding** work; **get / find / land / start / lose** a job; be **self-employed / one's own boss**; get a **promotion / pay rise**; take **a pay cut / early retirement**; get **fired / let go / the sack**; work **hard / tirelessly / together**

Unit 17

drift / drop off to sleep; **be fast / sound** asleep; **feel / look / sound / grow** sleepy; a **light / restful / long / deep / sound** sleep; sleep **soundly / well / tight**; a **heavy / light** sleeper; grab **a little shut-eye / some sleep**; have **an early / a late** night; have a **lie-in / nightmare**; press the snooze button; be a night owl; walk in one's sleep; from sun up to sun down; cry oneself to sleep

Unit 18

healthy **choice / food / heart / routine**; health **problems / benefits / concerns / risk / scare**; **exceptional / perfect / good / poor** health; **gentle / daily / regular / aerobic / strenuous** exercise; **get / remain / stay** healthy; **become / fall / look** ill; **catch / get / have** a cold; **lose / gain** weight; get a **checkup / prescription / second opinion** make a **fast / speedy** recovery; call in sick; get (back) into shape; be over the worst of something; be on the mend

Unit 19

be **full of / overcome by** emotion; **hide / suppress / bottle up** one's feelings; **express / show** one's emotions; be in **high spirits / a good / a bad** mood; be filled with **dread / concern**; **blissfully / deliriously / ridiculously** happy; **profoundly / unbearably** sad; **bitterly / hugely** disappointed; absolutely **delighted / exhausted**; deeply **saddened / offended / concerned**; utterly **disappointed / confused**; completely **exhausted / satisfied**; desperately **lonely / unhappy**; jump for joy; be tickled pink

Unit 20

fashionable / trendy / stylish clothes: **casual / dress / business / formal / smart** clothes: **old-fashioned / second-hand / vintage / retro / hand-me-down** clothes; **be in / set a / come (back) into / go out of** fashion; fashion **icon / show / magazine / statement / shoot / industry**; **casual / formal / modern / individual / personal / latest** style; designer **clothes / name**; dress **appropriately / fashionably / extravagantly**; follow a **trend / fashion**; **pale / bold / bright / brilliant / vibrant** colour; **delicate / rich / fine / light** fabric; the height of fashion

Unit 21

ask / give / tell someone the time; **(just) in / in the nick of** time; watch the **time / clock**; **lose / save / kill** time; **make / allow extra** time for something; **on / right on** time; have no time to **spare / lose**; time **flies / passes / goes by / is slipping away**; take **time / a day** off; **hectic / chaotic / laid-back** lifestyle; **hectic / demanding / gruelling / exhausting / packed** schedule; **plan / follow / revise / stick to** a schedule

Unit 22

good / exciting / fantastic news; **bad / shocking / terrible / awful** news; **yesterday's / front-page / breaking** news; **read / follow / catch up on** the news; news **story / headline / flash**; **daily / respectable / print** newspaper; **balanced / biased** story; **pitch / kill / bury** a story; **fair / balanced / comprehensive / round-the-clock** coverage; **anonymous / reliable** source; **banner / attention-grabbing / misleading** headline; **print / online / broadcast** journalist

Unit 23

family / chain / theme / self-serve restaurant; **cheap / hole-in-the-wall / elegant** restaurant; **daily / set / fixed-price** menu; **see / order from** the menu; **lunch / chef's / today's** special; **order / share / start with** an appetiser; **place an / put in an / take one's** order; **spoil one's / work up an** appetite; **light / heavy / simple / main / three-course** meal; **poor / terrible / friendly / excellent** service; **cosy / friendly / relaxed / warm / informal** atmosphere; dine **in style / al fresco**; leave a gratuity; add a service charge

Unit 24

protect / pollute / impact the environment; **endangered / protected** habitat; **finite / natural / renewable / sustainable** resources; **healthy / balanced / threatened** ecosystem; **man-made / natural** disaster; **energy / water / wildlife** conservation; **protected / threatened / invasive** species; **become / go** extinct; severe **drought / thunderstorm**; climate **denier / sceptic**; greenhouse **gas / effect**; be under threat

Unit 25

friendly / strong / harmonious relationship; **fragile / failed / troubled** relationship **serious / intense / long-term** relationship; **be in / work at / develop / break off** a relationship; **be / become / get** serious; **be / fall** in love; **have / start / get into** a fight; **be / stay / keep** in touch; lose touch with someone; have a crush on someone; ask someone out on a date; significant other; unrequited love

Unit 26

verbal / nonverbal / written / visual communication; **lines / channels / means** of communication; **brief / lengthy / serious / informal / personal** conversation; communicate **clearly / effectively / verbally / electronically**; speak **softly / loudly / clearly / eloquently / lovingly**; give a **lecture / seminar / talk**; **have / give / conduct** an interview; **have / get into / win / lose** an argument; **talk / speak / discuss** at length; **start / spread** a rumour; **engage / address** the listener; maintain eye contact; strike up a conversation; exchange pleasantries; use hand gestures

Unit 27

big **decision / surprise / failure / improvement**; large **amount / population / quantity / collection**; great **skill / detail / wealth / understanding / wisdom**; strong **feeling / emphasis / contrast / smell / taste**; deep **devotion / thought / sleep / depression / trouble**; heavy **fog / traffic**; **massive / high / sheer / substantial** number; **small / tiny / low / sufficient** number; **industrial / literary** giant; **decrease / reduce / increase** the size; **become / feel / look / get** fat; **become / feel / look / get** thin

Unit 28

joyous / noisy / quiet / family / special celebration; **public / religious / secular** holiday; **birthday / anniversary / housewarming / going-away / costume / fancy dress** party; **rich / family / local / religious** tradition; celebrate **a birthday / an anniversary**; dress up in **costumes / traditional clothes / fancy clothes**; join in the **celebration / festivities**; attend a **concert / play / festival**; perform a **song / dance**; watch **a parade / a performance / a show / fireworks**; **uphold a / break with** tradition; **say a / offer up a** prayer; **give / propose** a toast; **have / go on** a picnic; throw a party; ring in the new year; blow out the candles; family **get-together**

Unit 29

technological **breakthrough / innovation / revolution / progress**; **state-of-the-art / outdated / old-fashioned / labour-saving / obsolete/ latest / modern** technology; **develop / employ / invest in** technology; **low- / high-**tech; computer **literate / savvy**; upgrade one's **phone / computer / skills**; change one's **settings / password**; open a new **browser / page / file**; **write / send / fire off / receive / reply to** an email; **soft / hard** copy

Unit 30

save / conserve / produce / generate / harness / waste energy; **amount / form / source** of energy; **solar / wind / geothermal / hydroelectric / nuclear** energy; energy **use / needs / costs / production / resources**; pollution **levels / limits / standards**; **prevent / fight / combat / reduce / monitor** pollution; **exploit / deplete** natural resources; **major / heavy / high-tech** industry; **marginal / considerable / devastating / profound** impact; **harmful / toxic / noxious / carbon** emissions; **hazardous / toxic / commercial / industrial** waste; **air / water / soil** quality; pose a serious threat

Unit 31

business **meeting / lunch / trip / leader / deal**; **niche / successful** business; **start / set up / manage** a business; **drum up / generate** business; **impose / levy** taxes; maximise one's **earnings / profits**; take on **new business / employees / staff**; make **cutbacks / money / a calculation / a deal**; generate **ideas / capital / revenue / wealth**; implement **guidelines / policies / rules / an agreement**; allocate one's budget; seek investment corner the market; break into new markets; close a deal

Unit 32

easy / big / spending money; lend / borrow / pay back / invest / raise money; spend / earn / pay / cost a fortune; save for college / a house / retirement; spend wisely / freely / lavishly; splurge on a meal / a holiday / oneself; be low on /short on / strapped for cash; invest heavily / wisely / aggressively; pay with cash / by credit card; financial hardship / reward / responsibility; spare / hard-earned cash; fixed / tight / limited budget; be on a budget

Unit 33

crime level / statistics; petty / minor / violent / vicious / perfect crime; carry out a / charge someone with a / fight / tackle crime; habitual / hardened / convicted criminal; enforce / obey / uphold the law; lenient / minimum / maximum / severe / stiff / prison sentence; harsh / cruel / severe / corporal punishment; issue / receive a ticket; get / receive / impose / levy / risk a fine; go to / leave / be released from / be discharged from / escape from prison; be guilty of shoplifting / speeding / murder / a crime; find someone innocent / guilty; seek compensation / damages; be soft / tough on crime; be under arrest; be behind bars; reasonable doubt; life in prison

Unit 34

good / bad / disruptive / exemplary / (un) acceptable behaviour; behave (in) appropriately / (ir)responsibly / aggressively; use bad / inappropriate / offensive language; accept the results / consequences; act impulsively / sensibly; follow orders / directions; make assumptions / judgments; show thanks / appreciation; throw a fit / tantrum; spread a lie / rumour; cause / make trouble; show (dis)respect; strong work ethic; resist change; jump to conclusions; respect someone's personal space

Unit 35

radio / newspaper / magazine / pop-up / front-page advert; print / TV / radio / online / direct mail / social media advertising; get into / penetrate / capture the market; niche / shrinking / expanding / domestic / overseas market; place / show / take out / run an advert; advertising campaign / strategy / revenue / agency; promotional materials / flyers / products / campaign; pass out flyers / brochures; catchy tune / jingle / slogan; brand awareness / marketing / preference; junk mail / email; spam / trash / junk folder; mailing address / list; a surge in advertising / views

Unit 36

fine / graphic / abstract / contemporary / modern art; **performing / visual** arts; **amateur / professional** artist; **aspiring / talented / gifted / struggling / distinguished** artist; artistic **license / freedom**; art **gallery / colony / treasures / connoisseur; make / create / appreciate** art; attend **an opening / an exhibit; oil / water colour / still life** painting; receive a **poor / great / rave** review; bold expression of something

Unit 37

age of **exploration / discovery**; explore **fully / briefly / thoroughly; accidental / remarkable / surprising / unexpected / chance** discovery; **great / polar / intrepid** explorer; **plan / go on / join / fund / mount** an expedition; **silk / fur / slave** trade; space **race / probe / mission / flight / ship / program**; private **company / venture / enterprise / plane**; lunar **orbit / module / atmosphere / gravity / eclipse**; solar **system / flares / activity / eclipse**; launch a **satellite / rocket / boat; enter / go into / put something into** orbit

Unit 38

political **newcomer / novice / campaign / bias; launch / run** a campaign; **run for / resign from** office; **propose / sponsor / co-sponsor / veto / kill** a bill; **nominate / vote for** a candidate; **build / put together** a coalition; be the **frontrunner / underdog**; cast a **ballot / vote; close / landslide** victory; **one- / two- / multi-**party system; voter **turnout / suppression; strong / razor-thin** majority; politically (in)correct; hold a vote; play politics; take a poll; big government; election day

Unit 39

wry / black / dark / visual / self-deprecating / topical humour; **stand-up / slapstick / romantic** comedy; **old / good / funny / sick / tasteless / practical** joke; **slight / loud / big / polite** laugh; **wickedly / uproariously / hilariously** funny; **get to / say** the punchline; laugh **loudly / gently / heartily / hysterically**; be the butt of the joke; be in on the joke; crack a joke; play a joke on someone; make a joke out of something; make faces at someone; strike one as funny; play on words

Unit 40

global / fair trade; **global / emerging** markets; **fierce / cut-throat / stiff** competition;
lower / middle / upper class; **high / low** standard of living; **economic / world** superpower;
rich / poor / wealthy nation; outsource **manufacturing / workers**; economic **growth /
indicators**; national **pride / sovereignty**; trade **agreement / surplus / deficit**; industrialised
nation / economy / world; market **trends / forces**; multinational **corporation / relations /
agreement**; **go into / fall into / come out of** a recession; pay one's fair share of taxes

Appendix
Speaking and writing prompts

Some exams ask students to speak or write about a topic. These sample prompts can be helpful in practising and developing your productive skills. Try to use collocations in your responses to sound more natural.

Unit 1 Friends

Tell me about your best friend.
What's important in a friendship?
What's a good way to make new friends?

Unit 2 Family

Do you come from a big or small family?
What do you like to do with your family?
Is yours a typical family? If so, how? If not, why not?

Unit 3 Social media

What social media sites do you belong to?
How do you use social media?
What are some positive and negative aspects of social media?

Unit 4 Home

Describe your neighbourhood.
What is your house or flat like?
What type of home would you like to live in someday?

Unit 5 Academic life

Describe a typical day of a college student.
What do/did you study? Why did you choose that area of study?
What are some challenges of being a student?

Unit 6 Food

What kinds of food do you like and dislike?
Do you think you have good eating habits? Why or why not?
How have your eating habits changed over time?

Unit 7 Appearance

Describe the appearance of a family member.
Describe your appearance.
Are you happy with how you look? Why or why not?

Unit 8 Travel

Tell me about your last holiday.
What advice would you give someone who wants to travel abroad?
Describe your dream holiday.

Unit 9 Leisure

What do you do for fun?
Describe a perfect summer day. What would you do?
Think of a family member. What leisure activities do they do that you don't do?

Unit 10 Shopping

Do you enjoy shopping? Why or why not?
Compare the experience of buying things in a shop vs shopping online.
What are some ways to save money when shopping?

Unit 11 Abilities

What are you good at?

What skills are important to have these days?

Do you think some people are born with talent? Why or why not?

Unit 12 Weather

What's the weather like today?

What type of weather do you like and dislike? Why?

Describe a time when you experienced extreme weather.

Unit 13 Personality

Do you think you have a good personality? Why or why not?

Describe the personality of your best friend.

What are the best personality traits to have? What are the worst?

Unit 14 Nature

What do you like doing outdoors in nature?

Describe a natural wonder in your country. What's special about it?

Which natural wonder would you most like to see? Why?

Unit 15 Routines

Describe your typical daily routine.

How long does it take you to get ready and go to class each day? Why?

Who does the chores at your home?

Unit 16 Work

What jobs do the people in your family have?

How is the current job market where you live?

Describe your dream job.

Unit 17 Sleep

Did you sleep well last night? Why or why not?

How much sleep do you get during the week? At the weekend?

What do you do when you can't get to sleep?

Unit 18 Health

Are you generally happy with your health? Why or why not?

What do you think constitutes good health?

What advice would you give someone who wants to improve their wellness?

Unit 19 Emotions

Think of some news you recently heard. How did it make you feel?

Describe a time when you felt very happy or excited.

Describe a time when you felt very nervous or afraid.

Unit 20 Fashion

Are clothes important to you? Why or why not?

Describe your fashion style.

What are some ways to 'dress for success'?

Unit 21 Time

What do you enjoy spending time doing?

Do you feel like you have enough time in a day? Why or why not?

What are some ways for people to manage their time better?

Unit 22 News

Do you follow the news? Why or why not?

What ways of getting the news are popular these days?

What are some of the negative aspects of tabloid newspapers?

Unit 23 Dining out

What do you like and dislike about dining out?
Describe the last time you ate in a restaurant.
What makes for a nice dining experience?

Unit 24 Environment

Are you more optimistic or pessimistic about the future of our environment? Why?
What are some environmental challenges we are facing today?
What can everyday people do to help fight climate change?

Unit 25 Relationships

Describe your ideal partner.
What are some ways people meet other people in your country?
What makes for a healthy relationship with another person?

Unit 26 Communication

What are some ways people communicate with each other?
Do you think you are an effective communicator? Why or why not?
What advice would you give someone who wants to communicate better?

Unit 27 Size

What is your biggest accomplishment?
What responsibilities do you think corporate giants have to society?
What are some things someone might do to lose weight?

Unit 28 Celebrations

How do you celebrate your favourite holiday?
How do people in your country celebrate birthdays?
What's your least favourite holiday? Why?

Unit 29 Technology

What technology do you use on a daily basis?
How has technology changed over the past ten years?
What new technology would you like to see someday?

Unit 30 Energy

Name a type of energy. What are its downsides?
What renewable energy do you think holds the most potential? Why?
What are some ways everyday people can reduce their carbon footprint?

Unit 31 Business

What are some challenges of starting your own business?
Would you like to run your own business? Why or why not?
What are some things that would be good to have in a business plan?

Unit 32 Money

How important is money to you?
Do you think children should receive an allowance? Why or why not?
What are some advantages of teenagers getting a job and earning their own money?

Unit 33 Crime

Is crime a problem where you live? Explain.
What are some ways to punish people for breaking the law?
Why do you think some people turn to crime? How can they be helped?

Unit 34 Behaviour

Is it easy for you to make decisions? Why or why not?
Think of a time when you witnessed poor behaviour. What happened?
In terms of behaviour, what kind of person would you like to work for?

Unit 35 Advertising

What are some ways to advertise different products?
Think of a TV or online ad you found effective. What made it so?
What ways of advertising do you find don't work well on you?

Unit 36 Art

Do you like art? Why or why not?
Do you think you are artistic? Why or why not?
What can make a work of art interesting?

Unit 37 Exploration

Name a famous explorer. What did this person achieve?
Why do you think some people love exploring new places?
Would you ever consider taking a trip to space? Why or why not?

Unit 38 Politics

What do you like or dislike about politics?
Name a politician. What do you know about this person?
Do you pay attention to politics in other countries? Why or why not?

Unit 39 Humour

What makes you laugh?
Describe the last comedy you saw. Did you find it funny?
Do you think offensive jokes or those in poor taste are funny? Why or why not?

Unit 40 Globalisation

What are some popular foreign products in your country?
What does 'globalisation' mean to you?
What are some positive and negative aspects of globalisation?

Index
Main collocations

English Collocations in Context

Collocation	Unit	Collocation	Unit	Collocation	Unit
circle the globe	37	decent job	16	earn a living	31
clean one's teeth	15	declare a major	5	earn money	32
clear blue skies	12	decline in attendance	36	easy-going	13
climate change	24	deeply hurt	19	effective communicator	26
climate crisis	24	demanding schedule	21	elect a candidate	38
climb a mountain	14	demonstrate a mastery	36	electronic device	29
close friend	1	of something		emerging economy	40
closed-minded	13	deserve the attention	36	emerging technology	29
comment on threads	3	designer label	20	emotional well-being	18
commercial break	35	destroy a friendship	1	endangered species	24
commercially	30	develop a friendship	1	energy source	30
developed		develop a style	36	engage in a	26
commit a crime	33	develop an interest in	9	conversation	
common thread	36	something		entry-level position	16
communicate a	26	developed country	40	environmentally friendly	30
message		developing country	40	establish boundaries	18
communication skills	26	die-hard shopper	10	eternally grateful	19
competitive advantage	31	dissolve parliament	38	exceptionally friendly	1
confirm one's sources	22	divulge a secret	1	exchange gifts	28
considerable number	27	do a puzzle	9	express gratitude	28
control something	29	do an impression of	39	extended family	2
remotely		someone		extensive menu	23
convey information	26	do anything for a laugh	39	extensively explore	37
cook from scratch	6	do chores	15	extreme weather	12
corporate giant	27	do community service	33		
cram for an exam	5	do market research	31	face-to-face	26
crime wave	33	do one's makeup	15	conversation	
cross paths with	1	do something for fun	9	facial expression	26
someone		do the laundry	15	fair reporting	22
curl up with a good	15	do vigorous exercise	18	fake news	22
book		do volunteer work	28	fall asleep	17
cutting-edge technology	29	donate to charity	32	fall flat	39
		dormant volcano	14	familiar sight	30
daily routine	15	double date	25	family member	2
daily special	23	draw up a business	31	farming practices	24
dangerous criminal	33	plan		fashion forward	20
day-to-day work	16	dress the part	20	fast food	6
dead-end job	16	drive a turbine	30	feel dead to the world	17
debate issues	38	dry humour	39	financial literacy	32

English Collocations in Context

English Collocations in Context

Index
Collocation expansion

English Collocations in Context

English Collocations in Context

English Collocations in Context

Collocation	Unit	Collocation	Unit	Collocation	Unit
gesture of friendship	1	go bald	7	graduate student	5
get (back) into shape	18	go climbing	9	graduate studies	5
get a checkup	18	go extinct	24	graphic art	36
get a coffee	9	go for a bike ride	9	great detail	27
get a fine	33	go for a drive	9	great explorer	37
get a good deal	10	go for a run	9	great skill	27
get a job	16	go for a walk	9	great understanding	27
get a mortgage	4	go into a recession	40	great wealth	27
get a pay rise	16	go into orbit	37	great weather	12
get a prescription	18	go on a picnic	28	great wisdom	27
get a promotion	16	go on a diet	6	greatly resemble someone	7
get a second opinion	18	go on a holiday	8	greenhouse effect	24
get divorced from someone	2	go on a picnic	9	greenhouse gas	24
		go on a tour	8	group of friends	1
get engaged to someone	2	go on an adventure	9	group tour	8
get fat	27	go on an expedition	37	grow sleepy	17
get fired	16	go on the internet	3	gruelling schedule	21
get healthy	18	go online	3	guided tour	8
get into a fight	25	go out for lunch	9		
get into an argument	26	go out of fashion	20	habitual criminal	33
get into the market	35	go running	9	hand-me-down clothes	20
get let go	16	go shopping	9	hands-on experience	16
get lunch	9	go to bed	15	happy home	4
get married to someone	2	go to class	15	hard copy	29
get separated from someone	2	go to prison	33	hard work	16
		go to sleep	15	hard-earned cash	32
get serious	25	go to the office	15	hardened criminal	33
get the sack	16	go to work	15	harmful emissions	30
get thin	27	going-away party	28	harmonious relationship	25
get to the punchline	39	good behaviour	34	harness energy	30
gifted artist	36	good friend	1	harsh punishment	33
give a lecture	26	good health	18	have a barbecue	9
give a seminar	26	good joke	39	have a bite	6
give a talk	26	good news	22	have a blast	9
give a toast	28	gourmet food	6	have a child on one's own	2
give an interview	26	grab a little shut-eye	17	have a child out of wedlock	2
give someone the time	21	grab some sleep	17		
global market	40	graduate from high school	5	have a coffee	9
global trade	40			have a creative mind	13

English Collocations in Context

Collocation	Unit	Collocation	Unit	Collocation	Unit
individual style	20	know something		lengthy communication	26
industrial waste	30	by heart	5	lenient sentence	33
industrialised economy	40			let a flat	4
industrialised nation	40	labour-saving	29	level-headed	13
industrialised world	40	technology		levy a fine	33
industry giant	27	lack skills	11	levy taxes	31
informal atmosphere	23	lack talent	11	liberal attitude	13
informal communication	26	laid-back lifestyle	21	life in prison	33
innate talent	11	land a job	16	life skills	11
instant message	3	landslide victory	38	lifelong friend	1
intense relationship	25	language school	5	light fabric	20
international travel	8	large amount	27	light meal	23
intrepid explorer	37	large collection	27	light rain	12
invasive species	24	large population	27	light snow	12
invest aggressively	32	large quantity	27	light wind	12
invest heavily	32	larger-than-life	13	like a GIF	3
invest in technology	29	personality		like a meme	3
invest money	32	last-minute shopping	10	like a page	3
invest wisely	32	late-night shopping	10	like a photo	3
iron the clothes	15	latest style	20	like a post	3
issue a ticket	33	latest technology	29	like a video	3
		laugh gently	39	like an image	3
job perks	16	laugh heartily	39	limited budget	32
job satisfaction	16	laugh hysterically	39	lines of communication	26
job security	16	laugh loudly	39	literary giant	27
join an expedition	37	launch a boat	37	live with one's partner	2
join in the celebration	28	launch a campaign	38	live with one's	2
join in the festivities	28	launch a rocket	37	significant other	
joyous celebration	28	launch a satellite	37	live with one's spouse	2
jump for joy	19	learn something by heart	5	local tradition	28
jump to conclusions	34	learning event	3	long career	16
junk email	35	leave a gratuity	23	long-haul flight	8
junk folder	35	leave home	4	long-lost friend	1
junk mail	35	leave prison	33	long-term relationship	25
just in time	21	leftover food	6	look at the menu	6
keep a secret	1	leisure activities	9	look fat	27
keep in touch	25	leisure time	9	look ill	18
kill a bill	38	leisure travel	8	look old for one's age	7
kill a story	22	lend money	32	look one's age	7
kill time	21				

English Collocations in Context

Index – Collocation expansion

English Collocations in Context

Index – Collocation expansion

English Collocations in Context

Collocation	Unit	Collocation	Unit	Collocation	Unit
the height of fashion	20	trendy clothes	20	upload a video	3
theme restaurant	23	tropical climate	14	upload an image	3
threatened ecosystem	24	tropical region	14	upper class	40
threatened species	24	tropical zone	14	uproariously funny	39
three-course meal	23	troubled relationship	25	use a coupon	10
three-story home	4	trusted friend	1	use a discount code	10
throw a fit	34	try a bite	6	use a gift card	10
throw a party	28	try a new recipe	6	use a voucher	10
throw a tantrum	34	try out a diet	6	use bad language	34
tight budget	32	TV advertising	35	use hand gestures	26
tight family	2	two-bed one-bath home	4	use inappropriate	34
time flies	21	two-party system	38	language	
time goes by	21	typical afternoon	15	use offensive	34
time is slipping away	21	typical evening	15	language	
time passes	21	typical morning	15	utterly confused	19
tinned food	6	typical weekday	15	utterly disappointed	19
today's special	23				
token of friendship	1	unbearably sad	19	verbal communication	26
topical humour	39	uncaring attitude	13	veto a bill	38
torrential rain	12	under-graduate student	5	vibrant colour	20
tourist hot spot	8	unexpected discovery	37	vintage clothes	20
tourist trap	8	unfriend someone	3	violent crime	33
toxic emissions	30	unique personality	13	virtual event	3
toxic waste	30	university education	5	visual arts	36
trade agreement	40	unpredictable weather	12	visual communication	26
trade deficit	40	unrequited love	25	visual humour	39
trade school	5	update one's profile	3	vocational course	5
trade surplus	40	update one's status	3	volcanic crater	14
train travel	8	upgrade one's	29	vote for a candidate	38
trash folder	35	computer		voter suppression	38
travel abroad	8	upgrade one's phone	29	voter turnout	38
travel arrangements	8	upgrade one's skills	29		
travel deal	8	uphold a tradition	28	walk in one's sleep	17
travel destination	8	uphold the law	33	warm atmosphere	23
travel documents	8	upload a GIF	3	wash the clothes	15
travel on business	8	upload a meme	3	waste energy	30
travel plans	8	upload a page	3	watch a movie	9
travel the world	8	upload a photo	3	watch a parade	28
tremendous talent	11	upload a post	3	watch a performance	28

CPSIA information can be obtained
at www.ICGtesting.com
Printed in the USA
LVHW021930131022
730660LV00014B/90

9 781913 825669